ANTIGONE,

the most relevant of all Greek dramas
today, is the tragedy of a young woman
who willfully breaks the law of the land,
defying the man who is ruler. It is a classic
example of the use of confrontation in
public affairs, and sets a hideous
precedent for the consequences that
result when the Idealistic young feel
compelled to disobey laws they cannot,
in all good conscience, observe.

The text for ANTIGONE is taken from the widely
acclaimed University of Chicago editions of
The Complete Greek Tragedies, edited by David Grene
and Richmond Lattlmore.

The additional material has been prepared by
Walter James Miller, noted critic, author, and translator,
currently Professor of English at New York University.

Antigone

Edited by
DAVID GRENE
and RICHMOND LATTIMORE

With Supplementary Materials Prepared by
WALTER JAMES MILLER

WSP
Ⅲ WASHINGTON SQUARE PRESS · NEW YORK

ANTIGONE

Washington Square Press edition published November, 1970

Published by

L

Washington Square Press, a division of Simon & Schuster, Inc.,
630 Fifth Avenue, New York, N.Y.

WASHINGTON SQUARE PRESS editions are distributed in the
U.S. by Simon & Schuster, Inc., 630 Fifth Avenue, New
York, N.Y. 10020 and in Canada by Simon & Schuster
of Canada, Ltd., Richmond Hill, Ontario, Canada.

Standard Book Number: 671–46556–2.
Introduction by David Grene, and Sophocles: Antigone *copy-*
right, 1954, by The University of Chicago. Supplementary
material copyright, ©, 1970 by Simon & Schuster, Inc. All
rights reserved. Published on the same day in Canada by
Simon & Schuster of Canada, Ltd., Richmond Hill, Ontario.
This Washington Square Press edition is published by
arrangement with the University of Chicago Press.
Printed in the U.S.A.

CONTENTS

ANTIGONE

THE RELEVANCE OF *ANTIGONE* TODAY

by *Walter James Miller*

Hipsters and stockbrokers, philosophers and poets, psychoanalysts and students—almost everyone is "turned on" by *Antigone*. Why? It is easy to see how everyone can find at least an argument, at best an inspiration, in Lessing's *The Golden Notebook* or in Cleaver's *Soul on Ice*. But how can we explain the perennial popularity of a Sophocles play first produced twenty-five centuries ago?

The answer must be, in part, that *Antigone* is just as relevant, timely, and urgent for us today as *Soul on Ice* is. But then, Sophocles has been like that for generation after generation. The full answer is inescapable. Even in such an agonizing "long moment" as ours, even in such a painful groping period between millennia, we need some art already under momentum and so predictive that it becomes more urgent all the time. Simple as that. Because, reading *Antigone*, we find ourselves musing something like this:

Generation gap. (Gaping wider?)

"Do your own thing." (It will terrify many for reasons they honestly cannot understand.)

Law and order. (For whom, against whom? Funny, it's often law and order against some nice people like Antigone and her boyfriend.)

Civil disobedience as an answer to injustice. (A

recent policy statement of the National Council of Churches calls it "obedience to conscience or a higher law . . .")

"I just obeyed orders." (Boston Massacre, Dachau, Dresden, My Lai, Kent State University.)

Inventive genius. (Run amok.)

"Power corrupts. Absolute power absolutely corrupts." (Lincoln could play Teiresias, almost.)

Feminism. (Why is the human female, in her efforts to realize her full potential, such a threat to the human male? After all, even Plato wanted his philosopher-kings to mate with self-assertive, well-educated ladies!)

Those are some of our immediate associations, immediate applications, as we read the honest-as-now verse that Sophocles wrote for his troubled (and all honest) characters. But how about the aspects of the play that *seem* to have no relevance, except maybe for a specialist? How about all the mythological references, the strange conventions of chorus and messenger, the air thick with remote history and pagan polytheism? What value do these have for us today? It is our purpose to show that the more we know about Antigone's world, and about Sophocles' world, the more we will love *Antigone* as part of our world. We seriously believe that if you have room in your pack for only five books, you might add to *Soul on Ice* and *The Golden Notebook* not only Mailer's *The White Negro,* and Fromm's *The Art of Loving,* but also Sophocles' *Antigone.*

1. THE WORLD OF OEDIPUS AND ANTIGONE

The ancient Greek dramatist usually chose his situations from legendary materials he had inherited from generations of poets. Although the Greeks regarded these legends as

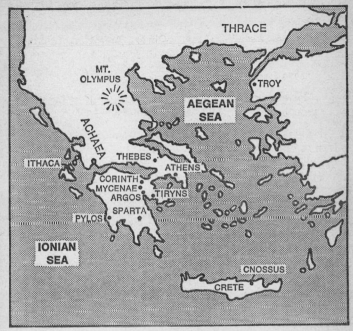

ANTIGONE'S WORLD
ca. 1300 B.C.

expressing historical truths, "rational" modern man tended, until recently, to think of them as fables. But decades of scientific research have now demonstrated that ancient myths do in fact reflect historical crises.

We know now that *Antigone* is based on events that took place in Thebes about the fourteenth or thirteenth century B.C. We know too that, in selecting and interpreting these Theban materials, Sophocles was representing problems of his own time and place: fifth-century B.C. Athens.

Hence *Antigone*, in addition to being a literary classic, proves to be a significant document in the history of ideas. And while its literary charm is hard to miss, its broad cultural value—archaeological, anthropological, psychological—

Wall of polygonal stones, Mycenae.   The Lion-Gate, Mycenae.
"Treasure House" of Atreus, Mycenae.

could be wasted on us unless we examine it in terms of Greek life and traditions.

In the sixteenth century B.C., a mixture of Mediterranean and northern peoples known as the Achaeans became the dominant power in the area we now call Greece. Their local rulers lived in massive walled fortresses built on high ground. Their chief ruler, or "king of men," reigned in Mycenae in south central Greece, where stone fortifications, beehive tombs, and the Lion Gate have all been excavated in recent decades. To the south stood the fortress towns of Argos, Tiryns, Sparta, Pylos; to the east, the citadel of Athens; and to the northeast, Thebes.

Built on a strategic ridge that separated two fertile plains, the great citadel of Thebes, known as the Cadmea, stood between the River Ismenus to the east and the River Dirce to the west (*Antigone*, lines 1123 and 102). Parts of three walls, unearthed on the site of modern Thebes, attest to the military might of Cadmea; relics such as a gold ring and artworks such as a fresco definitely link Theban culture with the Mycenaean world. Remains of a Theban building resemble Minoan structures found on the island of Crete, which the Mycenaeans absorbed into their empire around 1450 B.C.

Apparently the Mycenaean world was torn by civil war sometime around 1300, and no later than 1280 B.C. Archaeological evidence indicates that Thebes was sacked, and Greek traditions attributed the humbling of Thebes to an army of Argives (l. 15), that is, Achaeans from the Argos-Mycenae area. In any event, Thebans did fight side by side with other Achaeans in the Trojan War, which archaeology now dates about 1230 B.C.

Athene

Records of the founding and early history of Thebes are preserved in a mass of legends. Some of these figure in early Greek poetry. For example, Hesiod, in his *Works and Days* (about 725 B.C.), linked the sack of Thebes with the sack of Troy as part of Zeus's plan to destroy mankind. But let us concentrate on the Theban myths that figure in *Antigone*.

Founder of Thebes, the legends say, was Cadmus (l. 1152). On advice of an oracle, he followed a cow and where she sank down in exhaustion, he founded a city on the ridge near the

Ares

source of Ismenus and Dirce. Planning to sacrifice the cow to the goddess Athene, Cadmus sent his companions to fetch water from the Kastalian spring (l. 1130). Many of them were slain by a serpent or dragon (l. 123) before Cadmus could rescue them by crushing the reptile with a stone. After he completed his sacrifice to Athene, the goddess told Cadmus to sow the dragon's teeth in the soil. Where the teeth fell, armed men sprang up and fought each other until only five survived. These five joined Cadmus's forces. When the citadel of Thebes was completed, it was named Cadmea in honor of its founder.

Interpreted by modern scholars, this legend suggests that wandering Cadmus took over the site of Thebes from local people who had already weakened themselves in civil strife. The use of a sacred cow to pick the site of a temple was common practice in the ancient world; and a serpent often symbolized a rival religion. The goddess guiding Cadmus was the goddess of wisdom: her appearance symbolizes the coming of wisdom to Cadmus. Ancient heroes in all cultures always justified their decisions by saying they were divinely inspired.

Like all founding patriarchs, Cadmus was believed to have consorted freely with divinities: he married Harmonia, daughter of Ares the god of war (l. 139) and of Aphrodite the goddess of love (ll. 781–800). One of Cadmus's children was Semele (l. 1118), a girl so beautiful that Zeus himself appeared to her as a man, and wooed and won her. But when she was six months with child, she demanded to see Zeus in his full glory as a deity. Because he had promised to gratify her every wish, Zeus had to comply: but of course she was consumed by his Olympian lightning in what Sophocles calls her "miracle-death" (l. 1139). The child, however, was preserved by Zeus, and he grew up as Bacchus, patron god of Thebes (l. 1122). Under another of his many names— Dionysus—he was also worshiped in the theater in Athens, as we shall see.

Another of Cadmus's children, Polydorus, was direct ancestor of Antigone. Polydorus's son Labdacus founded the ruling house of Thebes (l. 592). His son Laius (l. 166) was warned by an oracle that he should remain childless unless he wanted to be killed by his

Zeus

own son. When King Laius nevertheless did sire a child, he and his wife Jocasta (l. 862) had it pinned through the feet and exposed on a mountain, the standard way of disposing of unwanted children in ancient Greece. But a sympathetic shepherd rescued the child and gave it to the childless king of Corinth, who—calling the boy Oedipus or "swollen-foot"—raised him as his own son.

Grown to manhood, Oedipus was told by an oracle that he would kill his father and marry his mother. Horrified, hoping to make the prophecy unfulfillable, he fled his home and his "parents" in Corinth; on the road to Thebes, he quarreled about the right of way with an older man, and fought and killed him. Arriving in Thebes, Oedipus saved the city from a sphinx and as a reward was given both the throne and the hand in marriage of the recently widowed queen, Jocasta. Unwittingly, Oedipus had killed his own father and married his own mother (ll. 855–864).

Only after he had sired two sons, Eteocles and Polyneices, and two daughters, Antigone and Ismene, did Oedipus discover that the prophecy had indeed been fulfilled. Jocasta hanged herself (l. 54); in shame, Oedipus blinded himself (l. 52) and wandered in exile, accompanied by his daughters, until he died at Colonus. The girls returned to live with their mother's brother, Creon (l. 531).

Meanwhile, Oedipus's sons had agreed to serve as kings of Thebes on alternate years. But when Eteocles' first year was nearly up, he issued an edict barring his brother from the throne. Polyneices went to Argos where he married a princess, and intent on regaining his rights, he mounted the expedition known as the Seven against Thebes. After heavy losses on both sides (ll. 100–150), Polyneices and Eteocles killed each other in single combat. The Argive army fled under cover of night (l. 15). Creon assumed the throne and issued the edict that provides the initial moment for Sophocles' play Antigone (ll. 158–192). For Creon ordered the people to bury Eteocles with full honors but to let Polyneices lie rotting on the field, prey to dog and vulture, as an object lesson for "rebels." But Antigone, acting out of "higher law," defiantly performed ritual burial of her brother. Creon, intent on crushing "civil disobedience" and restoring "law and order," decreed that Antigone be put to death.

Ironically, the Theban triumph celebrated in *Antigone* (ll. 148–153) was short-lived, for the sons of the seven who had fallen at Thebes now marched against Creon to avenge—and bury—their fathers. After another battle outside the city walls, the Thebans took the advice of the prophet Teiresias and abandoned their city, which the young Argives then sacked and looted.

How accurately these myths reflect the details of the political and military history of Thebes we may never know. With one qualification, however, we can say that these myths do fit into the general pattern of Theban history now being reconstructed by modern researchers. The qualification, of course, is that where a myth says "god" or "divine," we must read "hero" or "symbol," or "extraordinary" or "superhuman." For we know that all ancient peoples deified their ancestors, their deceased leaders, and the forces of both nature and human nature.

Many other Theban myths—such as those about Amphion (l. 1152) and Niobe (l. 825)—are also used by Sophocles, but how and why these legends figure in *Antigone* we shall consider in our discussion of dramatic techniques.

The dying hero—from pediment of a Greek temple

Sophocles

2. THE WORLD OF SOPHOCLES

Having looked into the thirteenth-century B.C. Mycenaean world in which Sophocles set his play *Antigone,* let us now consider the fifth-century B.C. Athenian world that produced Sophocles, the drama, and the playgoers.

Early in the fifth century the Greeks lived under the threat of conquest by the Persian armies of Xerxes. The Greeks regarded the Persian king—whom they called *the*

SOPHOCLES' WORLD
ca. 440 B.C.

Coiffures of Greek ladies

king—as the very type, the very symbol of absolute monarchy, of tyranny they despised. In 494 the armies of the eastern despot crushed the Greek colonies in Asia Minor, and in 490 a huge Persian force landed at Marathon, a day's forced march from Athens. With very little aid from the rest of Greece, the Athenians attacked; that night 6,400 Persians lay dead on the field, compared with 192 Athenians. But ten years later the Persians tried again; after overwhelming a valiant Spartan force at Thermopylae, the invaders lost a decisive sea battle at Salamis in 480 and a land battle at Plataea the following year.

The victorious Greeks now liberated their colonies in Asia Minor and punished Thebes, which had sided with the Persians—an important relationship for us to keep in mind. The question now was, How could the Greeks secure themselves from renewed Persian threats?

Their immediate solution was to form the Delian League, a voluntary confederacy of Greek city-states with headquarters in Athens and its treasury on the island of Delos. Each ally was to contribute either money or ships and crews. By mid-century, the league, carrying the wars to Asia and Africa, had forced the Persians to agree to respect the Greeks' territorial integrity.

In Athens, the immediate result of these triumphs was a brilliant burst of energy in every area of civic and cultural enterprise. Fortunately, Athens had the kind of government best suited for guiding this new creative power. For Athens was the world's first democracy. Its political system fostered freedom of thought and inquiry, and provided fertile soil for the growth of new ideas.

Athens was not a representative democracy like ours, but a direct democracy, requiring participation of every citizen in a "town-meeting" type of assembly. Officials were elected by the assembly for one-year terms; no man could be re-elected for the succeeding year except to the position of general. This was how Pericles, for example, stayed in power; but notice that he had to stand for reelection every year.

True, democratic rights were not extended to slaves, of whom there were about one hundred thousand in the metropolitan area. They did all the manual work in the silver mines and in the kitchen, at the plow and at the oar. But it is important to remember that all ancient civilizations were based on slavery; that the slave was usually a prisoner-of-war who, according to the ancient code of warfare, accepted slavery as a consequence of defeat; that in Athens slaves were treated very well, enjoying even the protection of the law. Democratic rights were denied to women too, even free women.

Greek ship

Pericles

Greek woman

But before we raise eyebrows about these limits on Athenian democracy, we must remember that in the United States, slaves were not freed until 1865, women not able to vote until 1920, and Blacks in many areas not able to vote with impunity until the 1960s. The main point here is that in a world of tyrants and despots, Athens invented democracy and extended it to all free males two thousand years before it was tried elsewhere.

The Athenian acted in person not only in legislative but also in judicial matters. He frequently served as a juror, often as a magistrate, and under no circumstances could he be represented by a lawyer: as plaintiff or defendant, he had to speak for himself. As a consequence, he took great interest in techniques of public debate and in political and philosophical issues that sharpened his intellect.

To meet this demand for "continuing education," as we would call it today, there emerged a class of professional teachers known as Sophists. *Their basic educational technique was to train their students to reexamine all fundamental issues, accepted and conventional ideas, "absolute standards," religious beliefs, and "authority." The Sophists encouraged discussion of the inalienable rights of the individual, the rights of private conscience as opposed to public compulsion, the privilege of human "nature" as opposed to society's "conventions." At the root of this growing philosophical inquiry was a supreme confidence in human intelligence as an instrument for probing ultimate truths.* Probably there never has been, anywhere, such a large citizenry so thoroughly trained to think so systematically and to perform with such versatility.

Still, somewhere, sometime, somehow, Athens made tragic mistakes. Failing to correct them before it was too late, too proud to admit her errors, she passed her peak of greatness almost before she reached it.

Symptomatic of Athens's sudden decline is what happened in the Delian League. Athens began to treat her allies as subjects. When Naxos and Thasos tried to withdraw from the league, Athens forced them to stay. What had once been their voluntary contributions to the Delos treasure now became their involuntary tribute! Indeed, in 454 B.C. the Athenians moved the treasury from Delos to Athens. Then they decorated Athens with new temples and statues paid for with Delian funds. Delian allies found large Athenian colonies planted in their midst to influence their courses of action. When Sophocles was elected general in 440 B.C., it was not to defend Greece from barbarous despots but to fight the Greek island of Samos, which had tried to withdraw from the unhappy Delian League. Samos was crushed. Athens, champion of freedom, had—in the name of freedom—crushed freedom.

Soon the most powerful members of the league were in

War chariot

open revolt—first Corinth, then Sparta, then others. Ironically, *the most democratic state was being punished by its
neighbors for interference in their affairs.* The imperialistic,
anti-democratic elements in Athens gradually threw their
support to Sparta. When Sophocles died in 406, Athens was
near collapse. Formal surrender did not come until 404 B.C.,
ending a glorious experiment in massive participation in the
life of the intellect.

Many critics have blamed the Sophists for Athens's fall,
pointing out that Sophism weakened absolute standards and
encouraged relativism and excessive individualism. Other
critics emphasize the fact that the pro-Sparta elements in
Athens worked hard to undermine Athenian democracy,
preferring, in some cases, to fight side by side with authoritarian Sparta. In any event, Athens was not the first nor the
last state to discover that power corrupts.

In considering how *Antigone* reflects actual historical
circumstances, we should remember then that—

• Athenians despised tyranny; for them, the name of the
  Persian king was a byword for tyrant;

• Fifth-century Thebes actually did ally herself with the
  Persians against the rest of Greece; hence in the
  Athenian mind, Thebans were associated with eastern
  despotism; *Antigone* is set in Thebes;

• Fifth-century Athenians were passionately interested
  in disputing fundamental questions such as the State
  versus the Individual Conscience;

• Sophocles, in his mid-fifties when he wrote *Antigone*,
  had had plenty of opportunity to see how even Athens,
  with the best (democratic) intentions in the world,
  could become a tyrannical and aggressive power.

3. SOPHOCLES' LIFE AND WORKS

About a mile northwest of Athens was a village called Colonus. It was, Sophocles himself tells us, a place "beloved of horsemen, . . . where leaves and berries throng, and wine-dark ivy climbs the bough, and the sweet . . . nightingale murmurs all day long." It was a place where narcissus and crocus bloomed, streams glided over the plain, and the olive, "fertile and self-sown, . . . blessed tree that never dies," mocked the soldier whose sword could not destroy it.

This lyric description, written for the chorus in his play *Oedipus at Colonus,* illustrates the close relationship between Sophocles' life, his world, and his writing. For Sophocles was born in Colonus, about 496 B.C. He was the son of Sophillus, well-to-do manufacturer of swords, spears, and armor. As a boy, Sophocles doubtless spent many hours in his father's shops, watching skilled carpenters, smiths, and armorers at their work. He always remembered—and used effectively—such telling details as the fact that (ll. 474-475)

> The strongest iron, hardened in the fire,
> most often ends in scraps and shatterings.

Greek shields

Greek swords and scabbards

And perhaps it was as a thoughtful adolescent, dreaming by the forge, that Sophocles first pondered the value and limits of man's "inventive craft" (ll. 332–372).

But Sophocles remembered his birthplace less as an industrial suburb and more as the haunt of Nature run wild, where he stored up unforgettable impressions of the eagle's outstretched wing, tracks of wild beast and hound, and sights and sounds around the carrion (ll. 30, 258, 307, 1113).

Although Sophillus was not a member of the aristocracy, he could still afford to give his son an aristocratic education. In fifth-century Athens, which, as we have seen, put a high premium on learning (ll. 710–711), the curriculum for boys stressed music, dancing, and athletics. Sophocles studied

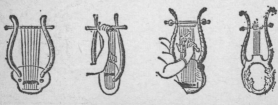

Forms of the lyre

music—essential for a Greek planning to write for the theater of Dionysus—under the celebrated Lamprus, who favored a severe, restrained style of composition. Sophocles was "crowned"—that is, graduated at the head of his class—in both music and athletics. Apparently he did well in dancing class too because all his life he was admired for his graceful movement.

At the age of seventeen, Sophocles was chosen to lead the chorus that celebrated the Greeks' naval victory over the Persians at Salamis. Standing around the trophies of the battle, the boys sang a paean—or hymn of thanksgiving—while Sophocles accompanied them on the harp. No boy was ever chosen for this honor unless he was handsome as well as talented.

Then Sophocles entered on a double career—on the one hand, that service in civic and military affairs required of all Athenian males, and on the other hand, his duties as a devotee of poetry and drama. It will help us understand the relations between his life and his writing if we consider his public service first.

A Greek discus-thrower

When he was eighteen, Sophocles donned "brazen arms" (l. 143) for two years of compulsory military training. In Greece this meant both land and sea service, so that Sophocles learned not only how to defend his "town with champion spear" (l. 195), but also how to control a ship in a storm (ll. 715–717).

Beginning with his twentieth year, Sophocles doubtless sat in "council-session" (l. 160) of the Athenian assembly, later serving on juries and committees, likely always to be elected to high office. In 443–442 B.C., he was president of the board that collected tribute from member states of the Delian League. In 440 he was one of ten military commanders elected to conduct the war against Samos; tradition has it that he won this election because of his popularity as the author of *Antig-*

one. The senior commandant was Pericles who—through regular reelection to this board of *strategoi*—was the guiding spirit of Athens during what we now think of as the Periclean Age (461–429 B.C.). Frequently thereafter Sophocles served on embassies to foreign lands and on public commissions at home. In short, government was the concern of every citizen: often in Sophocles' plays the point is made that "No city is property of a single man" (l. 737).

Asklepios

Sophocles was also active in the spiritual life of Athens. He was a founder of the cult of Asklepios, a mortal associated with the arts of healing who had been deified after his death. Temples of Asklepios were used for "incubation," a religious rite that required a sick person to sleep in the temple and then tell his dreams to the priest-physicians. After listening to these dreams, the "sons of Asklepios" believed themselves better able to administer to the patient. Sophocles held a priestly office in this cult and composed a famous paean to Asklepios that was sung in Athens for two hundred years. In *Antigone* too Sophocles rejoices in the power of medicine (ll. 360–361).

Here the reader will see that Sophocles was clearly interested in what we would now call psychosomatic medicine, the psychology of dreams, and the working of the unconscious. This interest is reflected in his plays in which often he uses a rapid series of images of an almost purely free-associational nature. Note also his admiration for human beings who could earn the reverence due a god (ll. 834–836).

The popular dramatist was notoriously susceptible to romantic passion. The famous choral ode in *Antigone* about the power of love "with whom no man can fight" was obviously based on personal experience (ll. 781–800). He was married at least twice that we know of and had at least five children. All that has come down to us about his immediate family indicates that Nicostrata, his first wife, was mother of Iophon, who became a tragedian like his father, and of Sophocles the Younger; Theoris, a later wife, bore him a son named Ariston. That we have no record of all the children is typical of ancient biography, which rarely mentions the relatives of a distinguished man unless they figured prominently in his career. Females especially were ignored; we have said nothing because we know nothing of his mother or of whether he had sisters. The typical Athenian woman was as cooped up as Eurydice appears to be in *Antigone;* when she did assert herself in public affairs, she was liable, like Antigone, to provoke the harsh contempt of the male supremacist.

Popular, affable, life loving, Sophocles knew virtually everyone of any importance in Athens. His intimate friends included Socrates the philosopher, Pericles the statesman, Herodotus the "Father of History," Ion the poet from Chios, Polygnotus the painter, and both his older competitor in the theater, Aeschylus, and his younger rival, Euripides.

Socrates and Plato

Sophocles participated in the vigorous intellectual life of a century in which men deliberately reexamined their basic concepts of man's nature and his relation to State, Truth, and Ultimate Reality. The tone of these philosophical discussions can be suggested with a few quotations from famous teachers of the period. Socrates is supposed to have said, *The unexamined life is not worth living.* Protagoras the Sophist taught that *Man is the measure of all things* and that *With regard to the gods, it is impossible to tell whether they exist or what they are like.* Hippias went further, saying that *Religion is a man-made device for en-*

Bust of Euripides

forcing morality through fear and *Laws are the convention of an older generation.*

That Sophocles was seriously challenged by these questions is clear in his plays. *Oedipus the King,* for example, is stamped with the impact of religious doubts. And the distinction between man-made laws and individual (religious) conscience figures prominently in *Antigone,* in which a young girl says to a king (ll. 453–456):

> Nor did I think your orders were so strong
> that you, a mortal man, could over-run
> the gods' unwritten and unfailing laws.

Of course, there were many in Athens who felt that the typical Sophist, such as Protagoras, was a "wicked teacher," as Creon says in *Antigone,* who "drives solid citizens to acts of shame" (ll. 298–299).

A Sophocles play was first produced in 468 B.C., when he was twenty-eight or twenty-nine. We can be sure it was not the first play he had written. Competition in Greek dramatic festivals (there were two in Athens alone) was rugged and a writer had to be an experienced artist to have a play accepted. Euripides, for example, was submitting plays for twelve years before he had his first one produced (at the age of thirty). Although the distinguished Aeschylus was competing in the Great Dionysia contest of 468, it was Sophocles who won the first prize.

Triptolemos, as this initial success was called, is not one of the Greek plays that have

Demeter and Persephone consecrating Triptolemus

Eleusinian priest

survived, but from the title we can infer the subject. Triptolemos was the Prince of Eleusis who was sent throughout the world by Demeter, earth goddess, to teach man the secrets of agriculture (ll. 1120–1121). This myth, on which Sophocles' play was obviously based, was also the main myth behind the Eleusinian Mysteries, a religious cult near Athens. At the height of the Eleusinian initiation ceremonies, the initiate was shown an ear of corn that had been "reaped in silence." All such rituals attempted to establish a connection between the fertility cycle of winter-death-and-spring-renewal and death-and-resurrection for man. For readers of *Antigone,* perhaps the main interest here is that from his earliest plays, Sophocles favored the earth goddesses.

Another lost play of interest to us is *Nausicaa.* Clearly it was about the sweet young princess of Phaeacia who was playing ball with her friends on the beach when the shipwrecked Odysseus was sleeping nearby. In Greek drama (as in Elizabethan drama), female parts were played by young men. Sophocles himself played Nausicaa and earned praise for the grace with which he imitated a girl. He did not have a very powerful voice, which is usually given as the reason he played girls' parts and the reason he subsequently gave up acting altogether.

Composing about 125 plays in all, and competing in thirty-one festivals, Sophocles won first prize at least eighteen times. This record compares with Aeschylus's thirteen first prizes and Euripides' three. But it is fair to point out that Aeschylus died young at sixty-eight, Euripides lived less than eighty years, and Sophocles was still writing plays at the age of ninety-one.

In the spring of 406 B.C., Sophocles heard that Euripides

Aeschylus

had died abroad. When Sophocles and his chorus next appeared in the theater of Dionysus, they were dressed in mourning. That autumn, Sophocles himself passed away. He was buried in the family vault, a mile from Athens on the road to Deceleia, near the nightingales. His tomb became an Athenian shrine, where annual sacrifices were made and the dramatist was worshiped as a hero.

Only seven of Sophocles' plays have come down to us in their entirety, but there are about a thousand passages —some of them up to twelve or fifteen lines long—quoted by other ancient writers that prove that at one time most of his plays must have circulated widely in manuscript.

Of the seven complete plays extant, the three that concern us most are the so-called Oedipus plays based on the Theban material we have already reviewed. These are—in the order of their composition—*Antigone*, produced in 441 B.C. when Sophocles was fifty-five; *Oedipus the King*, produced when he was seventy-five; and *Oedipus at Colonus*, produced posthumously by Sophocles' grandson in 401 B.C. Considering these plays in the historical order of their content, we see that *Oedipus the King* dramatizes that day in the Oedipus story when he discovers he has unwittingly killed his father and married his mother; his daughters, Antigone and Ismene, appear briefly and mutely at the end of this tragedy. In *Oedipus at Colonus,* the exiled and purified Oedipus is received by the gods in a miraculous hero-death; Antigone and Ismene figure prominently in this play. And the last part of the story of that ill-fated family, *Antigone,* is concerned with that day when King Creon orders the "rebel" Polyneices left unburied, the day when Antigone disobeys the king in order to obey her conscience. (A fuller discussion of the relationships among these Theban plays will be found in David Grene's essay, pp. oo–ooo.)

Speaking from our knowledge of 7 of his 125 works, we can say that Sophocles was concerned mainly with man's efforts to find his own identity; with the relation between good and evil and between a man's strengths and his weaknesses; and with the struggle of the individual conscience to relate to the power of the State. The two plays that best represent these questions are the perennial favorites, *Oedipus the King* and *Antigone.*

4. THE THEATER OF SOPHOCLES

Like democracy, theater was an Athenian idea. And among many cultural experiments that reached their peak in fifth-century Athens, drama was one of the most influential.

In *Antigone,* Sophocles reminds us of the origins of Greek drama. The elders sing of Bacchus whom they describe as (ll. 1118–1151)

> Leader in dance of the fire-pulsating stars,
> overseer of the voices of night,
> child of Zeus, . . .
> with due companionship of Maenad maids
> whose cry is but your name.

Bearded Dionysus and Satyr

Bacchus, or Dionysus, god of wine and revelry, was thus conceived of as leader of a troop of wild dancers— *maenads* (literally, mad girls) and *satyrs* (goatlike woodland demons).

Long before Sophocles' time, the annual spring festival

Maenad

of Dionysus had been celebrated by a group called a *chorus* (the word in Greek means *dance*, a meaning best preserved in our word *choreography*). The leader of the chorus was masked and dressed as Dionysus, the others as his attending maenads and satyrs. They sang stories about the exploits of the god of the vine.

About 536 B.C., Thespis, a choral leader, conceived the idea of the *actor*, another masked performer who did not dance or sing but *spoke:* he conversed with the leader and the group. Probably Thespis's new dramatic chorus first performed in the Rural Dionysia (outside Athens) but in any event he is credited with producing the first formal tragedy at the City Dionysia, inside Athens, about 534 B.C. Later, a second actor was added, probably by Aeschylus, who began producing his plays in Athens in 499 B.C. And it was Sophocles who is credited with adding the third actor.

More actors meant more dialogue, and the role of the chorus was correspondingly reduced until a tragedy became more dramatic than choral. The subject matter of the dramatic portions was broadened to include any mythological or historical material, the connections with Dionysus being preserved mainly in the choral and ritual elements.

In 441 B.C., when *Antigone* was first performed, the theater was still a kind of temple, the performance still nominally an act of worship of Dionysus, now more widely regarded as the god of vitality. The greatest Greek theater was the theater of Dionysus, which could seat about fifteen thousand spectators in a hollowed-out hillside in Athens. Virtually at the center of the theater was an altar, at which religious sacrifices were performed before the play. Around the altar was a circular area for the chorus, who thus revolved around the presence of the god as they danced. Arranged outside the dancing area, for three-quarters of the circle, were marble seats rising upward and outward like the steps of a modern stadium. The remaining ninety degrees of the circle—the front of the theater—was devoted to the stage proper. This consisted of a two-story building *(skene)* in the background, which, viewed externally, served as palace, residence, or temple, as required, and which, internally, contained dressing rooms for actors; and a flat

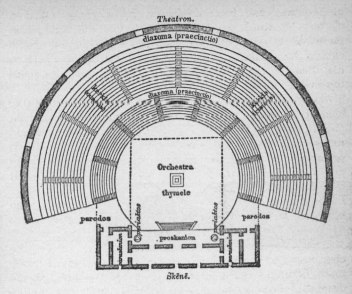

Plan of a Greek theater

stage area in front of the building *(proscenium)*, which
served as street, court, or garden. (That all action took
place out-of-doors was natural to the Greeks, who conducted
all business in the open air and designed their homes to
get as much direct light, ventilation, and view of sky as
possible.)

Plays were presented over several (three to six) days in
March. For each of the first three days, the program included a *tetralogy*, or group of four plays by one author.
The tetralogy consisted of a group of three tragedies, or a
trilogy, followed by a *satyr play*, a brief comedy or farce.
Originally the trilogy comprised three connected plays, but
by Sophocles' day playwrights could offer three plays on
separate subjects. The satyr play, in which the chorus
dressed like Dionysian revelers, served two purposes: it
provided a comic "chaser," and it concluded the tetralogy
on a Dionysiac note.

After 486 B.C., full-length comedies were added to the

Dionysia: they were performed either one a day after the tragic tetralogy, or in succession on the succeeding day or days. The audience, who appeared at sunrise, included the population at large except for soldiers on duty and baby-sitters. They brought cushions and food, prepared to stay until sunset. The seats of honor, down front, were reserved for public officials, priests, and judges of the dramatic contests.

A trumpet sounded to command silence. The first actors entered from a door of the building and conversed on the proscenium; the chorus would enter (l. 100) from one side through the *parodos* or the space between the *skene* building and the marble seats.

The play proceeded with alternating appearances of the actors in *episodes* and the chorus in *stasima* (choral odes). About five such alternations (ten parts) constituted a play (giving rise later to the conventional five-act play).

Actors wore large masks, depicting types such as a young girl (e.g., Antigone), young man (Haemon), and old woman (Eurydice). These masks made it possible for people in the back rows (three hundred feet away!) to recognize the characters: masks also made it possible for the same actor to take several roles in the same play. Hence, in *Antigone*

Masks 1-4 used in tragedy.   Mask 5 used in Satyric dramas.
Masks 6-10 used in comedy.

one actor could wear a helmeted mask to play the guard and later return wearing an old man's mask to play Teiresias.

At the end of the festival, the judges—who had been chosen by lot to serve as a civic duty—awarded first, second, and third prizes to the competing poets; and prizes to the producer (*choragus*) of the best play and to the star actor (*protagonist*). The playwright did not expect to gain money, only honor. The producer was a wealthy man who paid all the expenses as a public service (in Athens, wealth had its obligations that no rich man could escape: for example, he went to war on a horse supplied and maintained by himself). The actors and the choral singers, who underwent long and expensive training, were paid for their performances and rehearsals. Choice of judges by lot was not so incongruous as it would seem today. Every Athenian, we should recall, strove to develop his critical taste and was quite experienced in appreciating poetry and ideas. Furthermore, the judges doubtless paid careful attention to audience reaction, so that their selections were very likely a reflection of popular opinion as well.

Plays introduced in the City Dionysia in March might be produced later in the Lenaea, a three-day festival held in January; in the Rural Dionysia; or in the courts of foreign nobles. After Sophocles' death, fifth-century plays were frequently revived.

As the theater developed over the centuries—from Thespis's time to the Romans'—it changed considerably. Many modern notions of what classical drama was like are thus valid for only a part of that long period in cultural history. It will be valuable then to discuss here a few common notions that do *not* apply to the time when *Antigone* was first produced:

• The grotesquely exaggerated masks we sometimes see used as symbols of tragedy and comedy do *not* resemble masks used in Sophocles' day; the belief that Sophocles' masks were made to function as megaphones has never been verified;

- The buskin, or shoe with high sole, worn to give an actor greater dignity, was developed *after* Sophocles' day;

- The belief that fifth-century dramatists were bound by the so-called unities of time and place, and that they did not present bloody horrors on stage, has no basis in fact. Sophocles, for example, does change the scene in his *Ajax;* there are several surviving plays in which scenes are spaced out over a long period of time; and still others in which bloody spectacles are presented on the proscenium: Ajax impales himself on his sword; Oedipus appears with eye sockets dripping blood; Philoctetes screams in agony over a bloody, ulcerated foot, and falls unconscious.

5. SOPHOCLES' STYLE AND DRAMATIC TECHNIQUES

We have seen that myth, a dancing chorus, and the alternation of choral singing and actors' dialogue were all built into Greek drama by its very nature and its history. Now let us consider how Sophocles uses these conventional, ritual elements to unfold his story of *Antigone.* What artistic capital does he make of them? To what extent does a poet like Sophocles add *poetic* elements to the *dramatic?*

MYTH AND IRONY IN SOPHOCLES

Myth served the Greek dramatist in several important ways. In the first place, it solved for him the artistic problem of *exposition.* The modern playwright loses much time —and risks boring his audience—as he sketches in the background of his characters, their situation, time, and place.

Even a great dramatist like Shakespeare is sometimes forced to use such lame devices as having one character tell the story of his life—before the action can proceed!

But Sophocles is fortunately above and beyond that. In the opening line of *Antigone,* one actor calls the other "My sister, my Ismene." Ten lines later, Ismene calls the first actor "Antigone." Immediately the audience, with its common knowledge of Greek myths, knew that the subject had something to do with the Oedipus family of Thebes. Five lines later, the audience knew the exact point in the family saga at which the action is taking place: the father, mother, and brothers are all dead, the Argive army is fled, the first Theban campaign is over.

You will say, Why go to see a play when you know the story, the outcome? How can you be surprised? Where is the suspense? What novelty is there to hold your interest?

And it is true that the modern dramatist or TV writer relies greatly on surprise, novelty, revelation. It is also true that you still go back to see a good movie a second or even a third time. Why, if you already know the story?

Because when we are familiar with the overall situation —as the majority of the Greek audience always was—we

Greek helmets

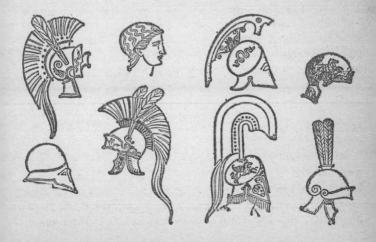

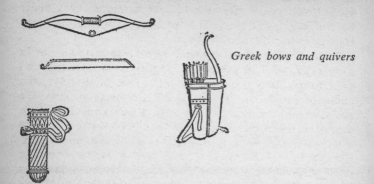

Greek bows and quivers

enjoy a different, deeper kind of suspense called *dramatic irony*. Because we know more than any character in the play knows, we now observe closely the way he acts in his ignorance, and everything he says means more to us than it means to him!

For example, Creon cannot appreciate the full significance of his own remarks when he declares (ll. 175–177):

> You cannot learn of any man the soul,
> the mind, and the intent until he shows
> his practise of the government and law.

Later, when he observes that "rigid spirits are the first to fall" (l. 473), he is unwittingly characterizing himself, the real Creon that will emerge in a crisis of government. Sophocles, famous for his excruciating exploitation of dramatic irony, pushes the device to its full artistic potential in passage after passage such as (ll. 677–680)

> . . . I must . . .
> not let myself be beaten by a woman.
> Better, if it must happen, that a man
> should overset me.
> I won't be called weaker than womankind.

Indeed, in his rigid refusal to yield to Antigone's point of view, Creon guarantees that he *will* be beaten by a man: by the very nature of the situation, it will be his son Haemon who will punish Creon.

Such effective use of dramatic irony puts the audience in a superior, godlike position. Knowing past, present, and even future facts unknown to the people in the play, the audience can follow the action on two levels at once. We are involved emotionally in the blind struggles of a character much like ourselves; for indeed, in real life we are all blind in that same way, forced always to act decisively without complete knowledge. Yet we can remain partly detached from his efforts, able to make judgments, to ponder man's pathetic predicament. In helping us appreciate the difference between appearance and reality, dramatic irony enables us—briefly at least—to transcend our own existence.

But myth also calls for interpretation, and so—hearing Antigone and Ismene identify themselves—a Greek audience would be interested in learning the significance that Sophocles attaches to their story. And each dramatist, in reinterpreting a myth, would vary the details and emphasize different aspects of the legend, so that minor surprises were added to the suspense already fostered by irony.

In addition to choosing a central myth on which he based his plot, Sophocles could draw freely on the entire body of Greek mythology to provide emotional overtones, analogies, comparisons, and explanations of ultimate causes.

A simple example of the power of the mythic allusion is Antigone's line, "Acheron is my mate" (l. 815), which would evoke, in the Greek mind, the horrible image of Antigone embraced by the grim figure who ferries the dead across the river Styx (l. 812).

Because the play deals with the conflict over Antigone's right to bury a brother who had died attacking his native city, the characters frequently refer to Zeus, guardian of kindred, who dwells on Mount Olympus (ll. 602, 657–658), and to divinities of the world of the dead (ll. 1201–1202). These references are intended to invoke religious awe and add mystery to the proceedings. Much more effective, though, are frequent allusions to the dread mother goddesses: Gaea, "the greatest of the gods, the earth" (l. 338); Demeter, the corn-mother (l. 1121); Persephone, whose winter life with her husband Hades, god of the underworld, and spring visit to her mother, Demeter, determined the alternation of the seasons (ll. 654, 894). To displease the *mother goddesses, who protect the life processes and revere life above man-made law,* is to tamper with Nature itself. And Creon, the Greek audience would believe, is offending these deities both by his refusal to return the dead to the earth and by his contempt for womanhood. "The Furies sent by Hades," the mother-avenging spirits that Teiresias says will haunt Creon, are especially identified with goddesses of the earth (l. 1076).

Both Antigone and the chorus explore the significance of her plight by free association to archetypal legends. Antigone, herself a princess of Upper Thebes, is sentenced to be imprisoned in a rocky cave (l. 774) and will never be a queen. She compares and contrasts herself with Niobe, Tantalus's daughter (l. 825) who became a queen when she married Amphion, King of Lower Thebes (l. 1152).

Erinys binding Pirithous in Hades. The Furies were actually a Roman adaptation of the Greek Erinyes.

Niobe

Niobe, who bore Amphion fourteen children, boasted she was more fruitful than the goddess Leto, mother only of the god Apollo and the goddess Artemis. Leto's children punished this blasphemy by killing Niobe's children; Niobe herself was turned into a rock. A stone mountain-face in Phrygia, which resembles a woman's face, was believed in ancient times to be Niobe: the melting snow and the rain pouring down across her features were, of course, her tears (l. 830).

Thinking still of that awful tomb in which Antigone will be buried alive, the chorus is reminded of other mythical figures who suffered horrible fates, and draws a moral or a consolation from each (ll. 945–984). Danaë's father imprisoned her in a bronze tower to keep her from marrying because it was prophesied that a son of hers would kill his grandfather. But Zeus himself visited her in a shower of gold, and the prophecy was fulfilled: she bore the demigod Perseus who slew her father. Lycurgus, "the angry king," opposed the introduction of Maenad cults into Thrace and was imprisoned by Dionysus. And Phineus's new wife, annoyed that his sons by a former wife looked at her so resentfully, blinded them.

At this point, Sophocles is using psychological associations as rapidly and obliquely as any modern surrealist—the former wife, Cleopatra, was reared in a cave; the boys now lived in the dark cave of blindness; Antigone's father had put out his own eyes—but they are all linked for the chorus because they demonstrate that you cannot escape your fate and must accept suffering.

For Sophocles, then, myth solved the problem of *exposition;* made it possible for him to exploit his extraordinary talent for intensive use of *dramatic irony;* and provided suggestive *allusions* rich in *mood* and *analogies.*

THE STRUCTURE OF ANTIGONE

Now let us consider how Sophocles constructs a scene, advances the action, and uses the chorus to heighten his dramatic effects.

In his first scene (called a *prologue:* ll. 1-99), Sophocles presents the sisters in a surreptitious discussion of their uncle's edict. Antigone intends to flout the decree and do her duty to the dead; but Ismene, speaking as a citizen, will obey the king, and speaking as a woman, will yield to the power of men. They separate, Antigone contemptuous of what she considers her sister's ignobility, Ismene nevertheless protesting her love.

Notice how much the author has packed into this short scene! He has introduced his *theme* (family loyalty versus obedience to the state) in terms of conflict on several levels. There is the *collision of ideas,* which provokes a *collision of personalities;* there is also a strong hint of impending *sexual antagonism.* And the scene ends with the two characters strongly contrasted and both *off-balance.*

The chorus in its first ode (called a *parodos:* ll. 100–153) hails the end of the siege; the elders want now to forget strife and celebrate peace with paean and dance. Their mood is in sharp contrast both to the feelings of the girls and to the state they will find themselves in very shortly. Already, then, in one alternation of actors and chorus, we have the main ingredients of drama: *conflict, contrast,* and *ebb and flow* of mood. And we already sense one function of the chorus—to represent broad public opinion as distinct from the views of the central characters. In performing this function, the chorus asks the question uppermost in the public mind (ll. 154–161), a question that directs our curiosity as Creon enters for the *first episode* (ll. 162–331).

After Creon promulgates his eloquent decree, we experience a brief but tense moment of *quiet drama:* while the chorus cautiously dissociates itself from the decree, even hinting that it concurs only under threat of death, Creon seems oblivious to what the lack of enthusiasm signifies. Then this moment of subtlety and deftness is followed by one of contrasting flat-footedness and ineptitude, as the poor guard reluctantly shambles in to deliver unwelcome news. His pathetically comic delivery sparks sudden and fierce conflict between Creon and chorus and then between Creon and guard, in the course of which the guard gains in dignity while Creon loses it. The very stuff of drama now: the *action seesaws* and *characters develop.*

As the episode ends, we realize that the chorus—which in many Greek plays simply observes and comments—is being used by Sophocles as an active character, that is, a human force that interacts with other characters. Then once again, this chorus, with its flexible perspective, in its first *stasimon* (ll. 332–372) takes a broad view of the situation. Apparently awed by the ingenuity that someone has displayed in accomplishing the forbidden rites, the elders muse on man's inventiveness but conclude that cleverness can be put to evil as well as to good use. And here we experience another moment of that deliberate ambiguity we have called dramatic irony: talking of the man who does these evil "things," the chorus doubtless means the unknown lawbreaker but the audience could be thinking instead of Creon the lawmaker.

Thus in each episode Sophocles explores a new conflict with a new *confrontation:* in episode two (ll. 373–581), Creon versus Antigone and Ismene; in episode three (ll. 630–780), Creon versus Haemon; in episode four (ll. 801–943), Antigone versus Creon; and in episode five (ll. 985–1114), Creon versus Teiresias. Each episode has its internal development, as, for example, when Haemon is driven from respectful reasonableness to rash fury; each episode further reveals the character of Creon; and each advances the play one step closer to its *crisis*. What we call the crisis is the turning point, in this case, the point at which Creon suddenly has the insight that makes him decide to undo what he has done.

Each episode has been followed by a stasimon in which the chorus has expressed some popular view: in stasimon two (ll. 582–623), that a family curse haunts great houses, and—a crucial idea in Greek thought—that power itself may bring doom; in stasimon three (ll. 781–881), that sexual love, like all great passions, can also bring ruin, and that Antigone's downfall is largely attributable to her own "daring" and "self-sufficiency"; in stasimon four (ll. 944–984), that one cannot escape fate. In stasimon five (ll. 1118–1151), after Creon has gone to bury Polyneices and free Antigone, the chorus prays that Bacchus, their protector, will come to the aid of their sick city. Their last-minute hope makes the tragic resolution all the more poignant.

Sophocles so contrives the final scene (called the *exodos*: ll. 1152–1352) that all the tragic consequences of the

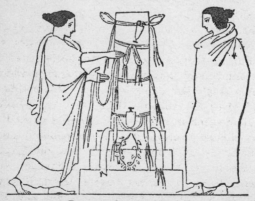

Decorated grave column

Creon-Antigone conflict are represented in rapid succession and dramatic buildup: first the tormenting piecemeal announcement; then the details of Antigone's suicide and of Haemon's attack on his father followed by his own suicide; then Creon—entering with his boy's body and cursing his own harshness—is hit with the final punishment, the vindictive suicide of his own wife.

The tragedy, of course, is that everything in this massive, seemingly incredible catastrophe has been credibly motivated, determined step-by-step by all-too-human action and interaction.

VARIATION OF VERSE FORMS

Although the musical quality of the verse can best be appreciated only in the original Greek, the way the *pacing* of the verse contributes to the movement of the play is perceptible even in translation.

This is easiest to detect in the choral odes, in which meaning is developed in neatly balanced strophes (groups of lines, stanzas). While each strophe adds a unit of thought, it also provides the measures for a part of the dance. In the original Greek, the patterns are often quite intricate, indicating a complicated choreography and swift changes of mood.

But the verse patterns are also artistically determined in the dialogue. As a scene develops, speeches vary in length. But as tension increases, Sophocles uses shorter speeches and finally *stichomythia*—dialogue in which *each speech is a single line of equal length.* This speeds up the pace and gives the action a fast, duellike, blow-for-blow quality. If the tension relaxes, the speeches expand. Notice that every climactic portion of each confrontation is rendered all or mostly in stichomythia, and that the greater the tension, the longer the stichomythic exchange: Antigone and Ismene (ll. 82–92), Creon and the guard (ll. 315–323), Antigone and Creon (ll. 508–523), Creon and Haemon (ll. 730–757), Creon and Teiresias (ll. 1049–1062).

6. SOPHOCLES' CHARACTERIZATION

In giving their new art form the name of *drama* (which in Greek means *action*), the Athenians meant to distinguish between a story that is told, as in a narrative poem, and a story that is acted out, as in a play. While all early dramatists used action to *reveal* character, Sophocles pioneered in the use of action to *develop* character. He so contrived a play that his characters face a predicament, a crucial situation that challenges them to prove themselves, to grow and change. We wonder, can they marshal all their strength and talents to resolve their difficulty? To what extent are they hampered by their own petty faults, their own blind spots? What will they (and we) learn as a result of their struggle with their inner as well as outer enemies?

In considering how Sophocles probes personality in depth, let us approach the main characters through the minor characters. We shall then be reminded of how the minor figures regard the central figures; we shall be better able to appreciate the people with whom the major characters must interact; and, because the lesser persons are more simply drawn, we may, in studying them first, find it easier to isolate some of Sophocles' techniques of characterization.

TREATMENT OF MINOR CHARACTERS

The chorus of elders, the palace guard, the high priest, and the messenger all serve to remind us how all life looks toward—and reflects events at—the king's palace.

The chorus of elders, as we have seen, represents the point of view of an average section of society. The elders are basically decent and well-meaning but not very profound or even adequate in crisis. Unable to give their hearty endorsement to Creon's decree, they content them-selves at first with muffled innuendoes and polite excuses (ll. 211–220). They are the first to suggest to Creon the religious implications of the dispute (l. 279), and they try to moderate between Haemon and Creon (ll. 724–725), but they are twice rebuffed and twice withdraw into silence. On the absolutely clear issue of Ismene's innocence, they are able to assert and win their point, but only after Creon, shaken by Haemon, feels troubled and needs support (ll. 769–771). They misinterpret Haemon's motives—attributing his defense of Antigone mainly to his love for her, over-looking Haemon's high-minded devotion to justice and principle (ll. 781–800). They weep for Antigone but they accept, blame her for, and abandon her to her fate (ll. 852–854, 875). Only when they learn that the high priest also sees Creon's act as offensive to the gods, only after Creon is *really* shaken (ll. 1094–1095), do they have the courage to tell Creon that he was "misguided" (l. 1104).

In other words, the chorus serves as an extreme contrast to the heroic personality. A hero is bold, individual, original; he acts on principle even at the risk of death. But the chorus is cautious, indecisive, discreet, conventional, more prone to follow than to lead; ultimately the elders prefer safety and survival. Hence we think of the chorus as a *foil* (we take the term from the jeweler's trick of placing a metal sheet behind a gem to enhance its luster), a foil for all the active, responsible, *committed* characters. The chorus, we fear, could well appear at a Nuremberg trial and say, "We just obeyed orders".

The guard is a cut above the elders in courage, several cuts below them in the scope of his wisdom. He also hesitates to face the trouble he has to face, but once insulted, he brazens it out with greater spirit and self-respect than all the chorus put together could muster (ll. 223–331). He has the decency to regret that his gain is Antigone's loss, the honesty to admit his relief that he is safe (ll. 437–440). Notice that his candid emphasis on personal survival (both his scenes end on that note) and his acceptance of a limited role in a world whose larger design he does not question help make him a somewhat comic figure. That he lives in fear of summary—even arbitrary—justice helps to characterize Creon. The king's first official "case" makes it clear that he is by no means a cool and impartial lover of objective inquiry. The way Creon treats the guard makes us apprehensive about Antigone's chances of being judged with mercy or even of being understood.

The only other "commoner" in the play, the messenger, is a stock character in classical drama who brings news of what has happened as the main characters move about offstage. But Sophocles uses every trick in his craft to save this walk-on from being a mere stick figure. The messenger tells his story in a very human way, first emphasizing the overall effect of the calamity on himself, making great proverbial capital out of it for others, coming to the facts only in jumbled hints, and finally giving a coherent account only when asked (ll. 1152–1243). Brief as his appearance is, it includes a *change*, and change—however slight—is the essence of life portrayal in literature. Puffed with his own importance, he opines that the queen "knows discretion. She will do no wrong" (l. 1250). But he is open to a different opinion and acts on it. The way he can tack gracefully in mid-course makes him a minor foil to the rigid Creon.

In another brief appearance, the high priest is also made to react in a way that tags him, a minor character, as a real person. A seer whose sayings—even Creon admits it —have always "been true," Teiresias represents an overall view of reality, a dimension that religion provides for man. He puts Creon's vengeance on a corpse into cosmic perspective as a mean and petty act. Yet he speaks in fatherly terms to the king, he is ready to understand and forgive, he can still see Creon as one who can cure "the trouble he has fallen in" (ll. 1023–1026).

But because Teiresias is human, there are limits to his magnanimity. When his counsel is rejected and his integrity attacked, he falters, sinks into dismay, and recovers with a slowness born of incredulity. Then the great power that has been used *for* Creon is raised *against* Creon. It is Teiresias who first uses the dread word *tyrant*. It is through

Teiresias that we first learn that not only Polyneices but *all* the seven lie unburied (ll. 1080–1081). And now himself humanly prone to vengeance, Teiresias adds to the threat of the Furies the spiteful remark: "Now say . . . I am bribed!"

Notice that Sophocles creates for every character the illusion of a full life lived before he comes on stage. In Teiresias's case he accomplishes this by having the king (and later the chorus) refer to the prophet's history; by having Teiresias himself speak with authority; by using provocative spectacle: the blind man led by a boy is accorded not the condescension due an invalid beggar but the awe due a great personage.

Sophocles' ability to endow a character with the aura of previous experience is demonstrated even in the smallest part of all. In terms of stage time, Eurydice is with us for merely a few minutes and speaks only seven lines (ll. 1180–1243). Here Sophocles has used the neat trick of keeping her offstage entirely until the last scene. Then—because we already know so much about her husband—her brief poignant request and her silent exit are all that are needed to suggest that this woman has suffered more than anyone from the character of Creon.

Thus we see, in Sophocles' treatment of these noncentral figures, that his main technique of character portrayal is to provoke a reaction, however slight, out of each member of the cast. Often, he makes the reaction of one character serve as illuminating contrast to the behavior of another character. He also makes one interaction, as between Creon and the guard, serve as a prelude, a foreshadowing for similar and more significant interactions, as between Creon and Haemon. He tags each member of the cast with some individual quality, and gives each some believable momentum of life already achieved.

DEVELOPMENT OF MAIN CHARACTERS

Now let us see how Sophocles combines these and other techniques to develop his four main characters in depth.

Ismene is a perfect foil. Her main dramatic function is
to illuminate Antigone's character by contrast. Ismene is
passive, obedient to the powers that be, a sweet girl who
pleads for a quiet life. Careful to motivate his characters,
Sophocles makes her yearnings understandable in the wake
of the catastrophes that have hit their family (ll. 49–58).
That the difference in their makeups has long been a bone
of contention between the sisters is implied repeatedly as
Ismene makes such statements as "You *crave* what can't
be done" (l. 90) and "I know that wild and futile action
makes no sense" (ll. 67–68). Ismene sums up the difference
to her own satisfaction when she calls Antigone "hard of
mind" (l. 47), and in that phrase she reveals how an
unambitious person regards a purposeful hero. Ismene, in
the first scene at least, is the "soft of mind" creature that
male supremacists (like Creon) expect women to be, and
Sophocles lets us see in Eurydice one fate in store for
such feminine submissiveness.

Yet, in an immature and neurotic way, Ismene does
love Antigone; pathetically Ismene realizes that without
Antigone she has no direction in her life (l. 567). She
accepts Antigone's action, just as we sense she has always
"gone along"; belatedly she wishes she had helped with
the heroic burial, and now she stands by her sister. Like the
guard, whose behavior prefigures hers, she has courage when
provoked. Still, she unconsciously reveals her ambivalence
or at least lack of self-motivation when she says to the
king (ll. 536–537):

> I did the deed, if she agrees I did.
> I am accessory and share the blame.

The clause *if she agrees* taints the confession as false and
neurotically blunts Ismene's intention. But aroused by
Creon's cruelty, Ismene falls back on her own particular
strength, the preservation of life: in four lines all of her
own motivation (ll. 568, 570, 572, 574) she protests the
sacredness of the tie between fiancé and fiancée. It is with
these lines that Ismene exposes some of the ugliest traits
in Creon.

Haemon is also a perfect foil, and a very dramatic one, for Sophocles is willing to have a son "show up" his father. In both what he says and how he says it, Haemon resembles the typical student of the Sophists. His entire presentation is well organized. He begins by reassuring his listener of his good intentions (ll. 635–638), thus encouraging Creon to describe his own feelings in a friendly atmosphere. Only then does Haemon raise his own argument, carefully stressing the way it benefits his listener: a king's son has his value to the king as a scanner of public reaction. As he proceeds, Haemon reflects Sophist views about the relativity and tentativity of all knowledge, the importance of reasoning not from preconception but from accumulated evidence, from hypotheses subject to revision.

Haemon wins every exchange with telling points: Creon, for example, is put in the position of rejecting correct logic simply because it comes from his junior. Ironically, it is not the king but the king's son who is revealed as more kingly: it is Haemon who stands for the dignity of both the people and the gods, while Creon, trapped into saying the city is his possession, is forced uncomfortably to shift ground (ll. 734–740). Creon stands for repressive authority, Haemon for democratic consensus. The final contrast between them consists in their attitudes toward women: Creon is infuriated at even the thought of an assertive woman, but Haemon is capable of loving one.

For full appreciation of Haemon's noble stature, we must note that he very scrupulously separates his political disagreement with his father from his personal interest in Antigone. Politically, he accepts constituted authority, even when he believes it has exceeded its rights, and he accepts the king's right to execute the lawbreaker (l. 751). Personally, he sees no alternative except to die with her. We are certain that if he were not in love with Antigone, he would defend her but of course not share her fate. His attempted violence against Creon, near the end, is not political but personal, and it would never have occurred if Creon had not come to the cave.

Antigone is one of the great character creations in world literature; only Shakespeare's Hamlet, Goethe's Faust, and

Sophocles' Oedipus have stirred more discussion, sympathy, and conjecture. How one looks at all four of these heroes depends largely on his time and place in the history of thought. Let us first review her action and see what it mainly indicates about her personality.

In comparing herself to Ismene, Antigone thinks of herself as "the doer." That she is an uncompromising idealist—one who *does* what she *believes*—is made clearer in the full context: "For me, the doer, death is best" (l. 72). For she prefers to die nobly than to survive ignobly; for her, to live while her brother's body is being chewed by the dogs is to survive in shame. Notice that this image dominates her thinking about her brother: she thinks first of the violation of his corpse (ll. 29-30) and secondly of the violation of religious law (ll. 73, 76-77). But for Antigone, private conscience, duty toward humanity, and religion are ultimately identical.

Although she is superhumanly single-minded in action, Antigone is humanly divided in her planning. On the one hand, her plans are based on Ismene's help, for she intends originally to lift and carry the body away (l. 43). On the other hand, she seems virtually certain Ismene will refuse to help: notice that Antigone starts to disparage Ismene even before detailing her plans (ll. 37-38):

> So there you have it and you soon will show
> if you are noble, or fallen from your descent.

At the very least, we must say that Antigone is totally lacking in the kind of tact that distinguishes Haemon; her intimidating approach is hardly calculated to win the delicate Ismene over to any bold exploits. In any event, Antigone's irritability and impatience are understandable because, with or without Ismene's help, she knows that she personally has embarked on a fatal enterprise.

When interrogated by the king, Antigone is again tactless, even calling him a fool. Is it again because she knows the kind of person she is dealing with and how hopeless it is to expect to be understood (ll. 450-470)? And when Ismene wants to share the blame, Antigone sees it not as evidence of Ismene's love but as Ismene's desire to gain a glory she does not deserve (l. 502). To the helpless Ismene, Antigone can only offer the bitter advice: "Love Creon" (l. 549).

In short, Antigone seems harsh toward anyone who does not condone her action. But she is not alone in this. It is typical, in time of crisis, for puritanical idealists to be extreme in this regard: "You are either with me or against me." And a heavy burden has been laid on this girl: with father and brothers dead, she undertakes the "masculine" responsibility of defending family and religious honor. She has, as we have seen, high standards of human dignity: how can she fail to be furious at Ismene, whose standards are feeble and flexible by comparison?

But then a very dramatic change occurs. When we next meet Antigone, she has softened. She laments now the marriage she will not live to enjoy (ll. 813–814) and the fact that she has "no friend to bewail" her fate (l. 881). She wonders whether the gods have forsaken her but she reflects that if she is wrong, she will see her error in suffering (ll. 922–927).

Then, in the midst of this mournful self-pity—which she has every right to savor now that her selfless task has been accomplished—she makes another statement that can be considered harsh. She would never, she says, have defied the law for a husband or for a child because she could always find a new mate or bear another child; but because her parents are dead, she can never have another brother. "Such was the law by which I honored" Polyneices (l. 912). This statement shocks some critics so much they think it has been inserted by another hand than Sophocles'.

Perhaps we should recall that at this moment she herself has no knowledge of whether Haemon, her erstwhile husband-to-be, has sided with her or with his father; while she mentions marriage frequently, she never mentions Haemon. Is she bitter at the uncertainty of romantic ties compared with the certainty of blood ties? Or is she rationalizing, as people always do, finding additional arguments for an action already taken? Such logic-chopping was typical of logic-loving Athens. As a matter of fact, an argument about family loyalties, similar to Antigone's "law," can be found in the writings of Herodotus, friend of Sophocles.

Antigone's position in these "shocking" lines can be seen as essentially a *matriarchal* position. A matriarchal society stresses blood ties, natural bonds, biology, worship of earth goddesses, humanity, and the sacredness of life itself. A *patriarchal* society stresses legal relations, marital ties, society itself, authoritarian gods, law above humanity. There can be no doubt that Sophocles was pointing out here that Antigone stands for the older, more humane matriarchal values, while Creon represents the later, more harshly logical and authoritarian system of the patriarchs. Modern psychoanalysts like Erich Fromm see in Sophocles' play a warning that humanity can destroy itself if it does not return to the more humane and "religious" values of matriarchy.

Again, is it really so shocking that Antigone should be contemplating extreme alternatives in a world that has forced extreme alternatives on her? She is the victim, not the creator, of a cruel dilemma that gave her a choice of breaking either a man-made (patriarchal) law or an earth-goddess (matriarchal) law. She was doomed if she did and doomed if she did not. And with a very beautiful sense of drama and human heroism, she chose to defy the tyrannical Creon rather than the cosmic Zeus.

Creon, the character exposed to greatest scrutiny, proves to be largely a study in irony. At the beginning, the Creon we see is *apparently* a decent man with decent values. But near the end, we see that Creon is *really* a puny and petty person, with no conception of the responsibility that goes with power. He is not totally evil—in his downfall he is able to see some of his mistakes—but he is that dangerous kind of personality whose weaknesses are first perceived as strengths. We have then in Sophocles' *Antigone* the kind of character study in which it is not only the main character, but also the audience's *perception* of the main character, that undergoes change. In Creon's case, we learn more than he does, because we feel that while he has been humbled he has not been ennobled.

Antigone's description of "the worthy Creon" (l. 31) does

not seem ironical to us at the start. His opening speech seems conventional in its premises—he stands for law and order—and admittedly he takes office under harrowing conditions. The country has been torn by civil war and the people yearn for peace and stability. While Creon's punishment of a corpse seems barbaric, taken in context it seems to be both an expression of wrath at Polyneices' treachery and an effort to end the war with an emphatic, symbolic gesture. The main point is, How will Creon handle the consequences of his decree and of the peace generally?

In his confrontation with the guard, we see him as a man already in trouble: he will not tolerate any difference of opinion (ll. 280–289); without evidence he suspects corruption among the people (ll. 294–301); and he cannot even keep his head. By his second entrance we get a rare introspective clue (l. 387): "What must I measure up to?" He himself finds it difficult to be a king! To the Greeks, he was by now already a familiar figure: like Agamemnon in the *Iliad*, Creon is the small man unable to handle a big job. But at least Agamemnon soon learned his weaknesses and begged his counselors to counsel him!

We definitely begin to take Creon's "measure" when he says (ll. 478–479):

Small curbs bring raging horses back to terms.
Slave to his neighbor, who can think of pride?

Here he expresses, consciously, the doctrine of iron control and, unconsciously, the authoritarian ruler's fear of the spirited personality. And he describes his own niece, daughter of the late king, as his slave!

Unable to be objective about persons with whom he has only a political relationship such as the guard and the elders, Creon is now put under the even greater strain of having to judge a close relative. He cannot be lenient with Antigone; that would be favoritism (ll. 486–490). Yet he unconsciously reveals a long-standing hatred of her which he does allow to figure in his judgment. And absolutely without grounds he charges Ismene with equal guilt. What he thinks is clever psychology (ll. 491–494)

> I saw her in the house,
> maddened, no longer mistress of herself.
> The sly intent betrays itself sometimes
> before the secret plotters work their wrong.

is to us just pathetic proof of his increasing paranoia. By the time Creon talks with his son, we see that the king is almost the perfect type of tyrant: *the ruler who uses the need for "good order" as his rationale for raw dictatorship.* The Athenians were quite familiar with the pattern: the famous "stability" of the nearby Spartan government was accomplished with suspicious repression of all individual liberty. And Sophocles carries this depiction of despotism to its excruciating extreme: Creon indulges his own worst sadistic tendencies, threatening to make his son watch his fiancée die. Modern man also is familiar with this pattern: Nazi Germany, to take just one example, explored many such subtleties of refined torture.

Teiresias's appearance offers Creon a chance to reverse himself without losing face; there is no disgrace in Greek life in following religious counsel, as Creon himself admits. Yet instead of taking a fresh look at the situation, Creon can only fit Teiresias into his original notion of conspiracy. In his fury he then commits an overt act of blasphemy when he says (ll. 1039–1041):

> . . . you will never cover up that corpse.
> Not if the very eagles tear their food
> from him, and leave it at the throne of Zeus.

For the Greeks, that is the signal that Creon is doomed: he has overreached himself. Whether one believes in the literal existence of Zeus or only in his symbolic value (as would the Sophists), one knows that Creon is willing to poison Nature itself rather than admit his error.

Still, when Creon finally capitulates (ll. 1113–1114)

> I've come to fear it's best to hold the laws
> of old tradition to the end of life.

we feel that it is only because Teiresias has added to the cosmic picture the threat of death in Creon's immediate family. Indeed, this feeling seems justified by the shocking spectacle of Creon's return—with Haemon's body only. To the end, he says nothing, does nothing, about his guilt toward Antigone.

For the Greeks, the tragedy was partly explainable in terms of two remarks uttered by the chorus (ll. 612–613; 1350–1351):

> one law controls them all:
> any greatness in human life brings doom. . . .

> Great words by men of pride
> bring greater blows upon them.

Creon, in short, was guilty of what the Greeks called *hubris*, arrogant pride, or the violent misuse of power.

7. THE RAW RELEVANCE IN SOPHOCLES

And so we see why *Antigone* has exerted such fascination down through the centuries: discussed by Aristotle, fussed over by Goethe and Hegel, warmly loved by Erich Fromm, a classic to the young in spirit in all ages.

First of all, we sympathize with Antigone and Haemon on the purely psychological level: we have all suffered in dilemmas, posed by the older generation, in which we were damned if we did and damned if we did not. Secondly, we sympathize with Antigone as a member of a second-class segment of society: she is a woman in a man's world, suffering double vengeance for her audacity in challenging her male "superiors." Thirdly, like Haemon, she is one of those brilliant, perhaps even precocious young people who have been most vindictively repressed for daring to think that youth has something to offer.

Fourthly, perhaps most significantly of all, *Antigone* is the first great artistic statement of a heroic stand that almost any person can be called upon to take just as a consequence of being a human being. Henry David Thoreau, Mahatma Gandhi, Martin Luther King are all following the example of Antigone when they take the position that (the words are Dr. King's) "Wherever *unjust* laws exist, people —on the basis of conscience—have a right to disobey those laws." In Nazi Germany and in Stalinist Russia, where to respect "law and order" was to violate the precepts of humanity, there must have been untold thousands of unsung Haemons and Antigones.

And so it can be no surprise to us that *Antigone* has an honored place in the typical hipster library, right next to Mailer's *The White Negro,* a modern version of the precept that "Laws are the conventions of an older generation," and Thoreau's *Civil Disobedience,* in which he says, "The only obligation I have a right to assume is to do at any time what I think right."

Finally, as citizens of a modern republic, we all sense the broader political allegory in *Antigone.* When Sophocles wrote the play in 441 B.C., he surely had in mind the greatness of Athens, her tragic indulgence in raw power, her failure to turn back in time. Twenty-four centuries later, after the Ahabs had begun their self-appointed task of policing the world, President Lincoln had to warn us, "Power corrupts. Absolute power absolutely corrupts." Sophocles was dealing, on all levels, with universal and timeless themes, with raw relevance.

ANTIGONE AND SOPHOCLES
IN HISTORICAL PERSPECTIVE

Historical Events	Dates (B.C.)	Literary Developments
Mycenaean Supremacy	1600–1200	Age of oral literature,
War against Thebes	ca. 1300	of mythology and oral
Trojan War	ca. 1230	epics
Greek Colonization of Asia Minor	1000–800	
	750–720	Homer: *Iliad, Odyssey*
		Hesiod: *Works and Days*
	ca. 534	Thespis: First Greek tragedy
	ca. 497	Sophocles born
Persian Wars	490–479	
	441	*Antigone* produced
Peloponnesian War (Sparta vs. Athens) begins	431	
	406	Sophocles dies
Athens surrenders	404	

INTRODUCTION TO
"THE THEBAN PLAYS" BY SOPHOCLES

by David Grene

This series of plays, *Oedipus the King, Oedipus at Colonus,* and *Antigone,* was written over a wide interval of years. The dating is only approximate, for reliable evidence is lacking; but the *Antigone* was produced in 441 B.C. when Sophocles was probably fifty-four, and *Oedipus the King* some fourteen or fifteen years later. *Oedipus at Colonus* was apparently produced the year after its author's death at the age of ninety in 405 B.C. Thus, although the three plays are concerned with the same legend, they were not conceived and executed at the same time and with a single purpose, as is the case with Aeschylus' *Oresteia.* We can here see how a story teased the imagination of Sophocles until it found its final expression. We can see the degree of variation in treatment he gave the myth each time he handled it. And perhaps we can come to some notion of what the myths meant to Sophocles as raw material for the theater.

The internal dramatic dates of the three plays do not agree with the order of their composition. As far as the legend is concerned, the story runs in sequence: *Oedipus the King, Oedipus at Colonus, Antigone.* But Sophocles wrote them in the order: *Antigone, Oedipus the King, Oedipus at Colonus.* In view of this and the long interval between the composition of the individual plays, we would expect some inconsistencies between the three versions. And there are fairly serious inconsistencies in facts, for instance. At the conclusion of *Oedipus the King,* Creon is in undisputed

authority after the removal of Oedipus. Though he appeals
to him to look after his daughters, Oedipus refrains from
asking Creon to do anything for his sons, who, he says, will
be all right on their own (OK 1460). It is Creon who will
succeed Oedipus in Thebes, and there is no question of any
legitimate claim of Oedipus' descendants (OK 1418). But in
Antigone, Creon tells the chorus that he has favorably
observed their loyalty first to Oedipus and then to his sons,
and so has hope of their devotion to himself. In Oedipus at
Colonus—the last of the three plays he wrote—Sophocles
makes one of his very few clumsy efforts to patch the dis-
crepancies together. In Oedipus at Colonus (ll. 367 ff.),
Ismene says that at first the two sons were willing to leave
the throne to Creon in view of their fatal family heritage,
but after a while they decided to take over the monarchy
and the quarrel was only between themselves as to who
should succeed. At this point Creon has vanished out of the
picture altogether! Again, the responsibility for the decision
to expel Oedipus from Thebes and keep him out rests, in
Oedipus the King, entirely with Creon, who announces that
he will consult Apollo in the matter. In Oedipus at Colonus
his sons' guilt in condemning their father to exile is one of
the bitterest counts in Oedipus' indictment of them (OC
1360 ff.). These are important differences. We do not know
anything really certain about the manner of publication of
the plays after their production. We know even less about
Sophocles' treatment of his own scripts. Maybe he simply
did not bother to keep them after he saw them as far as the
stage, though that seems unlikely. Or it is possible and
likelier that Sophocles, as he wrote the last play in extreme
old age and in what seems to be the characteristic self-
absorption of the last years of his life, cared little about
whether Oedipus at Colonus exactly tallied, in its presentation, with the stories he had written thirty-seven and
twenty-two years earlier.

Let us for the moment disregard the details of the story
and concentrate on what would seem to be the central
theme of the first two plays in order of composition. And
here we find something very curious. Most critics have felt
the significance of the Antigone to lie in the opposition of

Creon and Antigone and all that this opposition represents. It is thus a play about something quite different from *Oedipus the King*. And yet what a remarkable similarity there is in the dilemma of Creon in *Antigone* and Oedipus himself in the first Oedipus play. In both of them a king has taken a decision which is disobeyed or questioned by his subjects. In both, the ruler misconstrues the role of the rebel and his own as a sovereign. In both, he has a crucial encounter with the priest Teiresias, who warns him that the forces of religion are against him. In both, he charges that the priest has been suborned. There the resemblance ends; for, after abusing the old prophet, Creon is overcome with fear of his authority and, too late, tries to undo his mistake. In *Oedipus the King* the king defies all assaults upon his decision until the deadly self-knowledge which starts to work in him has accomplished its course and he is convicted out of his own mouth.

Usually, as we know, the *Antigone* is interpreted entirely as the conflict between Creon and Antigone. It has often been regarded as the classical statement of the struggle between the law of the individual conscience and the central power of the state. Unquestionably, these issues are inherent in the play. Unquestionably, even Sophocles would understand the modern way of seeing his play, for the issue of the opposition of the individual and the state was sufficiently present to his mind to make this significant for him. But can the parallelism between the position of Oedipus in the one play and Creon in the other be quite irrelevant to the interpretation of the two? And is it not very striking that such a large share of the *Antigone* should be devoted to the conclusion of the conflict, as far as Creon is concerned, and to the destruction of his human happiness?

What I would suggest is this: that Sophocles had at the time of writing the first play (in 442 B.C.) a theme in mind which centered in the Theban trilogy. One might express it by saying that it is the story of a ruler who makes a mistaken decision, though in good faith, and who then finds himself opposed in a fashion which he misunderstands and which induces him to persist in his mistake. This story is later on going to be that of a man who breaks divine law without realizing that he is doing so, and whose destruction is then brought about by the voice of the divine law in society. Between the *Antigone* and *Oedipus the King*, the theme has developed further, for in the latter play Sophocles is showing how the ruler who breaks the divine law may, for all he can see and understand, be entirely innocent, but nonetheless his guilt is an objective fact. In the third play, *Oedipus at Colonus*, this issue reaches its final statement. The old Oedipus is admittedly a kind of monster. Wherever he comes, people shrink from him. Yet his guilt carries with it some sort of innocence on which God will set his seal. For the old man is both cursed and blessed. The god gives him an extraordinary end, and the last place of his mortal habitation is blessed forever.

What this interpretation would mean, if correct, is that Sophocles started to write about the Theban legend, the story of Oedipus and his children, without having fully understood what he wanted to say about it. He may have been, and probably was, drawn, unknown to himself, to the dramatization of this particular legend because in it lay the material of the greatest theme of his later artistic life. But first he tried his hand at it in the opposition of Creon and Antigone. However, even while he did this, the character of Creon and his role in the play were shaping what was to be the decisive turn in the story he was going to write—the Oedipus saga.

Thus there is a certain elasticity in the entire treatment of myth. The author will accent a certain character at one time to suit a play and change the accent to suit another. Or he may even discover the same theme in a different myth. This is suggested by a short comparison of the *Philoctetes* and *Oedipus at Colonus*, both written in the last few years of Sophocles' life. The figure of Philoctetes, though occurring in a totally different legend from Oedipus, is a twin child with Oedipus in Sophocles' dramatic imagination. In both these plays, the *Philoctetes* and *Oedipus at Colonus*, the hero is a man whose value is inextricably coupled with his offensive quality. Philoctetes is the archer whose bow will overcome Troy. He is also the creature whose stinking infested wound moves everyone to disgust who has to do with him. Oedipus is accursed in the sight of all men; he had committed the two crimes, parricide and incest, which rendered him an outcast in any human society. But he is also the one to whom, at his end, God will give the marks of his favor, and the place where he is last seen on earth will be lucky and blessed. This combination of the evil and the good is too marked, in these two plays, to be accidental. It is surely the idea which inspired the old Sophocles for his two last plays. There is, however, an important further development of the theme in the *Oedipus at Colonus*. For there in Oedipus' mind the rational innocence—the fact that he had committed the offenses unknowingly—is, for him at least, important in God's final justification of him. Sophocles is declaring that the sin of Oedipus is real; that the consequences in the form of the loneliness, neglect, and suffering of the years of wandering are inevitable; but that the will and the consciousness are also some measure of man's sin— and when the sinner sinned necessarily and unwittingly, his suffering can be compensation enough for his guilt. He may at the end be blessed and a blessing. This is not the same doctrine as that of Aeschylus, when he asserts that through suffering comes wisdom. Nor is it the Christian doctrine of a man purified by suffering as by fire. Oedipus in his contact with Creon, in his interview with Polynices shows himself as bitter, sudden in anger, and implacable as ever. He is indeed a monstrous old man. But at the last, he is, in a measure, *vindicated*. Yet in *Philoctetes* the theme of the union of the offensive and the beneficial, which in *Oedipus at Colonus* becomes the curse and the blessing, is seen without the addition of conscious innocence and unconscious guilt. Can we say that Sophocles finally felt that the consciousness of innocence in Oedipus is the balancing factor in the story? That in this sense *Oedipus at Colonus* is the further step beyond *Philoctetes* in the clarification of the dramatic subject which occupied the very old author? Or that the consciousness of innocence when linked with objective guilt is only the human shield against the cruelty of the irrational—that Oedipus is meaningful in his combination of guilt and innocence as a manifestation of God and of destiny and that his explanation of his conscious innocence is only the poor human inadequate explanation? Everyone will answer this according to his own choice. But, clearly, the theme of Philoctetes and the theme of the old Oedipus are connected.

If an analysis such as this has importance, it is to show the relation of Sophocles to the raw material of his plays— the myth. It is to show the maturing of a theme in Sophocles' mind and his successive treatments of it in the same and different legends. In the Oedipus story it is a certain fundamental situation which becomes significant for Sophocles, and the characters are altered to suit the story. Creon in the first, Oedipus in the second, are examples of the same sort of dilemma, even though the dilemma of Creon in the *Antigone* is incidental to the main emphasis of the play, which is on Antigone. But the dilemma was to be much more fruitful for Sophocles as a writer and thinker than the plain issue between Antigone and Creon. The dilemma resolves itself in the last play at the end of Sophocles' life into the dramatic statement of a principle, of the union of the blessed and the cursed, of the just and the unjust, and sometimes (not always) of the consciously innocent and the unconsciously guilty. The fact that Sophocles could in two successive treatments of the play fifteen years apart switch the parts of Creon and Oedipus indicates that neither the moral color of the characters nor even their identity was absolutely fixed in his mind. The same conclusion is borne out by the great similarity between the *Philoctetes* and the *Oedipus at Colonus*. Sophocles in his last days was incessantly thinking of the man who is blessed and cursed. For the theater he became once the lame castaway Philoctetes, who yet, in virtue of his archery, is to be the conqueror of Troy; in the next play he is Oedipus, who sinned against the order of human society but is still to be the blessing of Athens and the patron saint of Colonus. It is the theme and not the man that matters. Consequently, it is the kernel of the legend, as he saw it for the moment, that is sacred for Sophocles, not the identification of all the characters in a certain relation to one another. True, he has treated the Oedipus story three times in his life, which means that the Oedipus story had a certain fascination for him -that somehow hidden in it he knew there was what he wanted to say. But he did not have to think of the whole story and the interdependence of its characters when he made his changes each time. One stage of the theme borne by the hero is given to a character in a totally different myth. The sequence is Creon, Oedipus, Philoctetes, Oedipus. It may seem absurd to link Creon, the obvious form of tyrant (as conceived by the Athenians), and Philoctetes. But it is the progression we should notice. The tyrant who with true and good intentions orders what is wrong, morally and religiously, is crudely represented in Creon; he is much more subtly represented in Oedipus himself in the next play. But the similarity of the situation and the nature of the opposition to him proves how generically the character is conceived. You can switch the labels, and Creon becomes Oedipus. But if the character is generic, the situation is deepening. We are beginning to understand *why* a certain sort of tyrant may be a tyrant and in a shadowy way how conscious and unconscious guilt are related. In the *Philoctetes* and *Oedipus at Colonus* the situation is being seen in its last stages. We are no longer concerned with how Philoctetes came to sin or how Oedipus is the author of his own ruin. But only how does it feel to be an object both of disgust and of fear to your fellows, while you yourself are simultaneously aware of the injustice of your treatment and at last, in *Oedipus at Colonus*, of the objective proofs of God's favor.

For Sophocles the myth was the treatment of the generic aspect of human dilemmas. What he made of the myth in his plays was neither history nor the kind of dramatic creation represented by *Hamlet* or *Macbeth*. Not history, for in no sense is the uniqueness of the event or the uniqueness of the character important; not drama in the Shakespearean sense, because Sophocles' figures do not have, as Shakespeare's do, the timeless and complete reality in themselves. Behind the figure of Oedipus or Creon stands the tyrant of the legend; and behind the tyrant of the legend, the meaning of all despotic authority. Behind the old Oedipus is the beggar and wanderer of the legend, and behind him the mysterious human combination of opposites— opposites in meaning and in fact. And so the character may fluctuate or the names may vary. It is the theme, the generic side of tragedy, which is important; it is there that the emphasis of the play rests.

ANTIGONE

CHARACTERS

Antigone

Ismene

Chorus of Theban Elders

Creon

A Guard

Haemon

Teiresias

A Messenger

Eurydice

ANTIGONE

SCENE: *Thebes, before the royal palace. Antigone and Ismene emerge from its great central door.*

Antigone
My sister, my Ismene, do you know
of any suffering from our father sprung
that Zeus does not achieve for us survivors?
There's nothing grievous, nothing free from doom,
not shameful, not dishonored, I've not seen.
Your sufferings and mine.
And now, what of this edict which they say
the commander has proclaimed to the whole people?
Have you heard anything? Or don't you know
that the foes' trouble comes upon our friends?   10

Ismene
I've heard no word, Antigone, of our friends.
Not sweet nor bitter, since that single moment
when we two lost two brothers
who died on one day by a double blow.
And since the Argive army went away
this very night, I have no further news
of fortune or disaster for myself.

Antigone
I knew it well, and brought you from the house
for just this reason, that you alone may hear.

Ismene
What is it? Clearly some news has clouded you. 20

Antigone
It has indeed. Creon will give the one
of our two brothers honor in the tomb;
the other none.
Eteocles, with just entreatment treated,
as law provides he has hidden under earth
to have full honor with the dead below.
But Polyneices' corpse who died in pain,
they say he has proclaimed to the whole town
that none may bury him and none bewail,
but leave him unwept, untombed, a rich sweet sight
for the hungry birds' beholding. 30
Such orders they say the worthy Creon gives
to you and me—yes, yes, I say to *me*—
and that he's coming to proclaim it clear
to those who know it not.
Further: he has the matter so at heart
that anyone who dares attempt the act
will die by public stoning in the town.
So there you have it and you soon will show
if you are noble, or fallen from your descent.

Ismene
If things have reached this stage, what can I do,
poor sister, that will help to make or mend? 40

Antigone
Think will you share my labor and my act.

Ismene
What will you risk? And where is your intent?

Antigone
Will you take up that corpse along with me?

Ismene
To bury him you mean, when it's forbidden?

Antigone
My brother, and yours, though you may wish he were
  not.
I never shall be found to be his traitor.

Ismene
O hard of mind! When Creon spoke against it!

Antigone
It's not for him to keep me from my own.

Ismene
Alas. Remember, sister, how our father
perished abhorred, ill-famed.   50
Himself with his own hand, through his own curse
destroyed both eyes.
Remember next his mother and his wife
finishing life in the shame of the twisted strings.
And third two brothers on a single day,
poor creatures, murdering, a common doom
each with his arm accomplished on the other.
And now look at the two of us alone.
We'll perish terribly if we force law
and try to cross the royal vote and power.   60
We must remember that we two are women
so not to fight with men.
And that since we are subject to strong power
we must hear these orders, or any that may be worse.
So I shall ask of them beneath the earth
forgiveness, for in these things I am forced,
and shall obey the men in power. I know
that wild and futile action makes no sense.

Antigone
I wouldn't urge it. And if now you wished
to act, you wouldn't please me as a partner.   70
Be what you want to; but that man shall I
bury. For me, the doer, death is best.
Friend shall I lie with him, yes friend with friend,

when I have dared the crime of piety.
Longer the time in which to please the dead
than that for those up here.
There shall I lie forever. You may see fit
to keep from honor what the gods have honored.

Ismene
I shall do no dishonor. But to act
against the citizens, I cannot.

Antigone
That's your protection. Now I go, to pile   80
the burial-mound for him, my dearest brother.

Ismene
Oh my poor sister. How I fear for you!

Antigone
For me, don't borrow trouble. Clear your fate.

Ismene
At least give no one warning of this act;
you keep it hidden, and I'll do the same.

Antigone
Dear God! Denounce me. I shall hate you more
if silent, not proclaiming this to all.

Ismene
You have a hot mind over chilly things.

Antigone
I know I please those whom I most should please.

Ismene
If but you can. You crave what can't be done.   90

Antigone
And so, when strength runs out, I shall give over.

Ismene
Wrong from the start, to chase what cannot be.

Antigone
If that's your saying, I shall hate you first,
and next the dead will hate you in all justice.
But let me and my own ill-counselling
suffer this terror. I shall suffer nothing
as great as dying with a lack of grace.

Ismene
Go, since you want to. But know this: you go
senseless indeed, but loved by those who love you.

> (*Ismene returns to the palace; Antigone leaves
>   by one of the side entrances. The Chorus
>   now enters from the other side.*)

Chorus
Sun's own radiance, fairest light ever shone on the
    gates of Thebes,   100
then did you shine, O golden day's
eye, coming over Dirce's stream,
on the Man who had come from Argos with all his
    armor
running now in headlong fear as you shook his bridle
    free.

He was stirred by the dubious quarrel of Polyneices.   110
So, screaming shrill,
like an eagle over the land he flew,
covered with white-snow wing,
with many weapons,
with horse-hair crested helms.

He who had stood above our halls, gaping about our
    seven gates,
with that circle of thirsting spears.
Gone, without our blood in his jaws,   120

before the torch took hold on our tower-crown.
Rattle of war at his back; hard the fight for the
   dragon's foe.

   The boasts of a proud tongue are for Zeus to hate.
   So seeing them streaming on
   in insolent clangor of gold,   130
   he struck with hurling fire him who rushed
   for the high wall's top,
   to cry conquest abroad.

Swinging, striking the earth he fell
fire in hand, who in mad attack,
had raged against us with blasts of hate.
He failed. He failed of his aim.
For the rest great Ares dealt his blows about,
first in the war-team.   140

   The captains stationed at seven gates
   fought with seven and left behind
   their brazen arms as an offering
   to Zeus who is turner of battle.
   All but those wretches, sons of one man,
   one mother's sons, who sent their spears
   each against each and found the share
   of a common death together.

Great-named Victory comes to us
answering Thebe's warrior-joy.
Let us forget the wars just done   150
and visit the shrines of the gods.
All, with night-long dance which Bacchus will lead,
who shakes Thebe's acres.

              (Creon enters from the palace.)

   Now here he comes, the king of the land,
   Creon, Menoeceus' son,
   newly named by the god's new fate.

What plan that beats about his mind
has made him call this council-session,   160
sending his summons to all?

Creon
My friends, the very gods who shook the state
with mighty surge have set it straight again.
So now I sent for you, chosen from all,
first that I knew you constant in respect
to Laius' royal power; and again
when Oedipus had set the state to rights,
and when he perished, you were faithful still
in mind to the descendants of the dead.
When they two perished by a double fate,   170
on one day struck and striking and defiled
each by his own hand, now it comes that I
hold all the power and the royal throne
through close connection with the perished men.
You cannot learn of any man the soul,
the mind, and the intent until he shows
his practise of the government and law.
For I believe that who controls the state
and does not hold to the best plans of all,
but locks his tongue up through some kind of fear,   180
that he is worst of all who are or were.
And he who counts another greater friend
than his own fatherland, I put him nowhere.
So I—may Zeus all-seeing always know it—
could not keep silent as disaster crept
upon the town, destroying hope of safety.
Nor could I count the enemy of the land
friend to myself, not I who know so well
that she it is who saves us, sailing straight,
and only so can we have friends at all.   190
With such good rules shall I enlarge our state.
And now I have proclaimed their brother-edict.
In the matter of the sons of Oedipus,
citizens, know: Eteocles who died,
defending this our town with champion spear,

is to be covered in the grave and granted
all holy rites we give the noble dead.
But his brother Polyneices whom I name
the exile who came back and sought to burn   200
his fatherland, the gods who were his kin,
who tried to gorge on blood he shared, and lead
the rest of us as slaves—
it is announced that no one in this town
may give him burial or mourn for him.
Leave him unburied, leave his corpse disgraced,
a dinner for the birds and for the dogs.
Such is my mind. Never shall I, myself,
honor the wicked and reject the just.
The man who is well-minded to the state
from me in death and life shall have his honor.   210

Chorus
This resolution, Creon, is your own,
in the matter of the traitor and the true.
For you can make such rulings as you will
about the living and about the dead.

Creon
Now you be sentinels of the decree.

Chorus
Order some younger man to take this on.

Creon
Already there are watchers of the corpse.

Chorus
What other order would you give us, then?

Creon
Not to take sides with any who disobey.

Chorus
No fool is fool as far as loving death.   220

Creon
Death is the price. But often we have known
men to be ruined by the hope of profit.

(*Enter, from the side, a guard.*)

Guard
Lord, I can't claim that I am out of breath
from rushing here with light and hasty step,
for I had many haltings in my thought
making me double back upon my road.
My mind kept saying many things to me:
"Why go where you will surely pay the price?"
"Fool, are you halting? And if Creon learns
from someone else, how shall you not be hurt?"   230
Turning this over, on I dilly-dallied.
And so a short trip turns itself to long.
Finally, though, my coming here won out.
If what I say is nothing, still I'll say it.
For I come clutching to one single hope
that I can't suffer what is not my fate.

Creon
What is it that brings on this gloom of yours?

Guard
I want to tell you first about myself.
I didn't do it, didn't see who did it.
It isn't right for me to get in trouble.   240

Creon
Your aim is good. You fence the fact around.
It's clear you have some shocking news to tell.

Guard
Terrible tidings make for long delays.

Creon
Speak out the story, and then get away.

Guard
I'll tell you. Someone left the corpse just now,
burial all accomplished, thirsty dust
strewn on the flesh, the ritual complete.

Creon
What are you saying? What man has dared to do it?

Guard
I wouldn't know. There were no marks of picks,
no grubbed-out earth. The ground was dry and hard,   250
no trace of wheels. The doer left no sign.
When the first fellow on the day-shift showed us,
we all were sick with wonder.
For he was hidden, not inside a tomb,
light dust upon him, enough to turn the curse,
no wild beast's track, nor track of any hound
having been near, nor was the body torn.
We roared bad words about, guard against guard,   260
and came to blows. No one was there to stop us.
Each man had done it, nobody had done it
so as to prove it on him—we couldn't tell.
We were prepared to hold to red-hot iron,
to walk through fire, to swear before the gods
we hadn't done it, hadn't shared the plan,
when it was plotted or when it was done.
And last, when all our sleuthing came out nowhere,
one fellow spoke, who made our heads to droop
low toward the ground. We couldn't disagree.   270
We couldn't see a chance of getting off.
He said we had to tell you all about it.
We couldn't hide the fact.
So he won out. The lot chose poor old me
to win the prize. So here I am unwilling,
quite sure you people hardly want to see me.
Nobody likes the bringer of bad news.

Chorus
Lord, while he spoke, my mind kept on debating.
Isn't this action possibly a god's?

Creon.

Stop now, before you fill me up with rage,   280
or you'll prove yourself insane as well as old.
Unbearable, your saying that the gods
take any kindly forethought for this corpse.
Would it be they had hidden him away,
honoring his good service, his who came
to burn their pillared temples and their wealth,
even their land, and break apart their laws?
Or have you seen them honor wicked men?
It isn't so.
No, from the first there were some men in town   290
who took the edict hard, and growled against me,
who hid the fact that they were rearing back,
not rightly in the yoke, no way my friends.
These are the people—oh it's clear to me—
who have bribed these men and brought about the
    deed.
No current custom among men as bad
as silver currency. This destroys the state;
this drives men from their homes; this wicked teacher
drives solid citizens to acts of shame.
It shows men how to practise infamy   300
and know the deeds of all unholiness.
Every least hireling who helped in this
brought about then the sentence he shall have.
But further, as I still revere great Zeus,
understand this, I tell you under oath,
if you don't find the very man whose hands
buried the corpse, bring him for me to see,
not death alone shall be enough for you
till living, hanging, you make clear the crime.
For any future grabbings you'll have learned   310
where to get pay, and that it doesn't pay
to squeeze a profit out of every source.
For you'll have felt that more men come to doom
through dirty profits than are kept by them.

Guard

May I say something? Or just turn and go?

Creon
Aren't you aware your speech is most unwelcome?

Guard
Does it annoy your hearing or your mind?

Creon
Why are you out to allocate my pain?

Guard
The doer hurts your mind. I hurt your ears.

Creon
You are a quibbling rascal through and through.   320

Guard
But anyhow I never did the deed.

Creon
And you the man who sold your mind for money!

Guard
Oh!
How terrible to guess, and guess at lies!

Creon
Go pretty up your guesswork. If you don't
show me the doers you will have to say
that wicked payments work their own revenge.

Guard
Indeed, I pray he's found, but yes or no,
taken or not as luck may settle it,
you won't see me returning to this place.
Saved when I neither hoped nor thought to be,   330
I owe the gods a mighty debt of thanks.

(*Creon enters the palace. The Guard leaves
by the way he came.*)

Chorus

Many the wonders but nothing walks stranger than
    man.
This thing crosses the sea in the winter's storm,
making his path through the roaring waves.
And she, the greatest of gods, the earth—
ageless she is, and unwearied—he wears her away
as the ploughs go up and down from year to year   340
and his mules turn up the soil.

Gay nations of birds he snares and leads,
wild beast tribes and the salty brood of the sea,
with the twisted mesh of his nets, this clever man.
He controls with craft the beasts of the open air,
walkers on hills. The horse with his shaggy mane   350
he holds and harnesses, yoked about the neck,
and the strong bull of the mountain.
Language, and thought like the wind
and the feelings that make the town,
he has taught himself, and shelter against the cold,
refuge from rain. He can always help himself.
He faces no future helpless. There's only death
that he cannot find an escape from. He has contrived   360
refuge from illnesses once beyond all cure.

Clever beyond all dreams
the inventive craft that he has
which may drive him one time or another to well
    or ill.
When he honors the laws of the land and the gods'
    sworn right
high indeed is his city; but stateless the man   370
who dares to dwell with dishonor. Not by my fire,
never to share my thoughts, who does these things.

(The Guard enters with Antigone.)

My mind is split at this awful sight.
I know her. I cannot deny
Antigone is here.

Alas, the unhappy girl,
her unhappy father's child.   380
Oh what is the meaning of this?
It cannot be you that they bring
for breaking the royal law,
caught in open shame.

Guard

This is the woman who has done the deed.
We caught her at the burying. Where's the king?

                         (Creon enters.)

Chorus

Back from the house again just when he's needed.

Creon

What must I measure up to? What has happened?

Guard

Lord, one should never swear off anything.
Afterthought makes the first resolve a liar.
I could have vowed I wouldn't come back here   390
after your threats, after the storm I faced.
But joy that comes beyond the wildest hope
is bigger than all other pleasure known.
I'm here, though I swore not to be, and bring
this girl. We caught her burying the dead.
This time we didn't need to shake the lots;
mine was the luck, all mine.
So now, lord, take her, you, and question her
and prove her as you will. But I am free.
And I deserve full clearance on this charge.   400

Creon

Explain the circumstance of the arrest.

Guard

She was burying the man. You have it all.

Creon
Is this the truth? And do you grasp its meaning?

Guard
I saw her burying the very corpse
you had forbidden. Is this adequate?

Creon
How was she caught and taken in the act?

Guard
It was like this: when we got back again
struck with those dreadful threatenings of yours,
we swept away the dust that hid the corpse.   410
We stripped it back to slimy nakedness.
And then we sat to windward on the hill
so as to dodge the smell.
We poked each other up with growling threats
if anyone was careless of his work.
For some time this went on, till it was noon.
The sun was high and hot. Then from the earth
up rose a dusty whirlwind to the sky,
filling the plain, smearing the forest-leaves,
clogging the upper air. We shut our eyes,   420
sat and endured the plague the gods had sent.
So the storm left us after a long time.
We saw the girl. She cried the sharp and shrill
cry of a bitter bird which sees the nest
bare where the young birds lay.
So this same girl, seeing the body stripped,
cried with great groanings, cried a dreadful curse
upon the people who had done the deed.
Soon in her hands she brought the thirsty dust,
and holding high a pitcher of wrought bronze   430
she poured the three libations for the dead.
We saw this and surged down. We trapped her fast;
and she was calm. We taxed her with the deeds
both past and present. Nothing was denied.
And I was glad, and yet I took it hard.

One's own escape from trouble makes one glad;
but bringing friends to trouble is hard grief.
Still, I care less for all these second thoughts
than for the fact that I myself am safe.   440

Creon
You there, whose head is drooping to the ground,
do you admit this, or deny you did it?

Antigone
I say I did it and I don't deny it.

Creon (to the guard)
Take yourself off wherever you wish to go
free of a heavy charge.

Creon (to Antigone)
You—tell me not at length but in a word.
You knew the order not to do this thing?

Antigone
I knew, of course I knew. The word was plain.

Creon
And still you dared to overstep these laws?

Antigone
For me it was not Zeus who made that order.   450
Nor did that Justice who lives with the gods below
mark out such laws to hold among mankind.
Nor did I think your orders were so strong
that you, a mortal man, could over-run
the gods' unwritten and unfailing laws.
Not now, nor yesterday's, they always live,
and no one knows their origin in time.
So not through fear of any man's proud spirit
would I be likely to neglect these laws,
draw on myself the gods' sure punishment.

I knew that I must die; how could I not?   460
even without your warning. If I die
before my time, I say it is a gain.
Who lives in sorrows many as are mine
how shall he not be glad to gain his death?
And so, for me to meet this fate, no grief.
But if I left that corpse, my mother's son,
dead and unburied I'd have cause to grieve
as now I grieve not.
And if you think my acts are foolishness
the foolishness may be in a fool's eye.   470

Chorus
The girl is bitter. She's her father's child.
She cannot yield to trouble; nor could he.

Creon
These rigid spirits are the first to fall.
The strongest iron, hardened in the fire,
most often ends in scraps and shatterings.
Small curbs bring raging horses back to terms.
Slave to his neighbor, who can think of pride?
This girl was expert in her insolence   480
when she broke bounds beyond established law.
Once she had done it, insolence the second,
to boast her doing, and to laugh in it.
I am no man and she the man instead
if she can have this conquest without pain.
She is my sister's child, but were she child
of closer kin than any at my hearth,
she and her sister should not so escape
their death and doom. I charge Ismene too.
She shared the planning of this burial.   490
Call her outside. I saw her in the house,
maddened, no longer mistress of herself.
The sly intent betrays itself sometimes
before the secret plotters work their wrong.
I hate it too when someone caught in crime
then wants to make it seem a lovely thing.

Antigone
Do you want more than my arrest and death?

Creon
No more than that. For that is all I need.

Antigone
Why are you waiting? Nothing that you say
fits with my thought. I pray it never will.   500
Nor will you ever like to hear my words.
And yet what greater glory could I find
than giving my own brother funeral?
All these would say that they approved my act
did fear not mute them.
(A king is fortunate in many ways,
and most, that he can act and speak at will.)

Creon
None of these others see the case this way.

Antigone
They see, and do not say. You have them cowed.

Creon
And you are not ashamed to think alone?   510

Antigone
No, I am not ashamed. When was it shame
to serve the children of my mother's womb?

Creon
It was not your brother who died against him, then?

Antigone
Full brother, on both sides, my parents' child.

Creon
Your act of grace, in his regard, is crime.

Antigone
The corpse below would never say it was.

Creon
When you honor him and the criminal just alike?

Antigone
It was a brother, not a slave, who died.

Creon
Died to destroy this land the other guarded.

Antigone
Death yearns for equal law for all the dead.

Creon
Not that the good and bad draw equal shares.   520

Antigone
Who knows that this is holiness below?

Creon
Never the enemy, even in death, a friend.

Antigone
I cannot share in hatred, but in love.

Creon
Then go down there, if you must love, and love
the dead. No woman rules me while I live.

   (*Ismene is brought from the palace under guard.*)

Chorus
   Look there! Ismene is coming out.
   She loves her sister and mourns,
   with clouded brow and bloodied cheeks,
   tears on her lovely face.   530

Creon
You, lurking like a viper in the house,
who sucked me dry. I looked the other way
while twin destruction planned against the throne.
Now tell me, do you say you shared this deed?
Or will you swear you didn't even know?

Ismene
I did the deed, if she agrees I did.
I am accessory and share the blame.

Antigone
Justice will not allow this. You did not
wish for a part, nor did I give you one.

Ismene
You are in trouble, and I'm not ashamed   540
to sail beside you into suffering.

Antigone
Death and the dead, they know whose act it was.
I cannot love a friend whose love is words.

Ismene
Sister, I pray, don't fence me out from honor,
from death with you, and honor done the dead.

Antigone
Don't die along with me, nor make your own
that which you did not do. My death's enough.

Ismene
When you are gone what life can be my friend?

Antigone
Love Creon. He's your kinsman and your care.

Ismene
Why hurt me, when it does yourself no good?   550

Antigone
I also suffer, when I laugh at you.

Ismene
What further service can I do you now?

Antigone
To save yourself. I shall not envy you.

Ismene
Alas for me. Am I outside your fate?

Antigone
Yes. For you chose to live when I chose death.

Ismene
At least I was not silent. You were warned.

Antigone
Some will have thought you wiser. Some will not.

Ismene
And yet the blame is equal for us both.

Antigone
Take heart. You live. My life died long ago.
And that has made me fit to help the dead.   560

Creon
One of these girls has shown her lack of sense
just now. The other had it from her birth.

Ismene
Yes, lord. When people fall in deep distress
their native sense departs, and will not stay.

Creon
You chose your mind's distraction when you chose
to work out wickedness with this wicked girl.

Ismene
What life is there for me to live without her?

Creon
Don't speak of her. For she is here no more.

Ismene
But will you kill your own son's promised bride?

Creon
Oh, there are other furrows for his plough.

Ismene
But where the closeness that has bound these two?   570

Creon
Not for my sons will I choose wicked wives.

Ismene
Dear Haemon, your father robs you of your rights.

Creon
You and your marriage trouble me too much.

Ismene
You will take away his bride from your own son?

Creon
Yes. Death will help me break this marriage off.

Chorus
It seems determined that the girl must die.

Creon
You helped determine it. Now, no delay!
Slaves, take them in. They must be women now.
No more free running.
Even the bold will fly when they see Death   580
drawing in close enough to end their life.

(Antigone and Ismene are taken inside.)

Chorus

Fortunate they whose lives have no taste of pain.
For those whose house is shaken by the gods
escape no kind of doom. It extends to all the kin
like the wave that comes when the winds of Thrace
run over the dark of the sea.
The black sand of the bottom is brought from the
     depth;
the beaten capes sound back with a hollow cry.   590

Ancient the sorrow of Labdacus' house, I know.
Dead men's grief comes back, and falls on grief.
No generation can free the next.
One of the gods will strike. There is no escape.
So now the light goes out
for the house of Oedipus, while the bloody knife   600
cuts the remaining root. Folly and Fury have done
     this.

What madness of man, O Zeus, can bind your power?
Not sleep can destroy it who ages all,
nor the weariless months the gods have set. Unaged
     in time
monarch you rule of Olympus' gleaming light.   610
Near time, far future, and the past,
one law controls them all:
any greatness in human life brings doom.

Wandering hope brings help to many men.
But others she tricks from their giddy loves,
and her quarry knows nothing until he has walked
     into flame.
Word of wisdom it was when someone said,   620
"The bad becomes the good
to him a god would doom."
Only briefly is that one from under doom.

(Haemon enters from the side.)

Here is your one surviving son.
Does he come in grief at the fate of his bride,
in pain that he's tricked of his wedding?   630

Creon
Soon we shall know more than a seer could tell us.
Son, have you heard the vote condemned your bride?
And are you here, maddened against your father,
or are we friends, whatever I may do?

Haemon
My father, I am yours. You keep me straight
with your good judgment, which I shall ever follow.
Nor shall a marriage count for more with me
than your kind leading.

Creon
There's my good boy. So should you hold at heart
and stand behind your father all the way.   640
It is for this men pray they may beget
households of dutiful obedient sons,
who share alike in punishing enemies,
and give due honor to their father's friends.
Whoever breeds a child that will not help
what has he sown but trouble for himself,
and for his enemies laughter full and free?
Son, do not let your lust mislead your mind,
all for a woman's sake, for well you know
how cold the thing he takes into his arms   650
who has a wicked woman for his wife.
What deeper wounding than a friend no friend?
Oh spit her forth forever, as your foe.
Let the girl marry somebody in Hades.
Since I have caught her in the open act,
the only one in town who disobeyed,
I shall not now proclaim myself a liar,
but kill her. Let her sing her song of Zeus
who guards the kindred.
If I allow disorder in my house

I'd surely have to licence it abroad.   660
A man who deals in fairness with his own,
he can make manifest justice in the state.
But he who crosses law, or forces it,
or hopes to bring the rulers under him,
shall never have a word of praise from me.
The man the state has put in place must have
obedient hearing to his least command
when it is right, and even when it's not.
He who accepts this teaching I can trust,
ruler, or ruled, to function in his place,
to stand his ground even in the storm of spears,   670
a mate to trust in battle at one's side.
There is no greater wrong than disobedience.
This ruins cities, this tears down our homes,
this breaks the battle-front in panic-rout.
If men live decently it is because
discipline saves their very lives for them.
So I must guard the men who yield to order,
not let myself be beaten by a woman.
Better, if it must happen, that a man
should overset me.
I won't be called weaker than womankind.   680

Chorus
We think—unless our age is cheating us—
that what you say is sensible and right.

Haemon
Father, the gods have given men good sense,
the only sure possession that we have.
I couldn't find the words in which to claim
that there was error in your late remarks.
Yet someone else might bring some further light.
Because I am your son I must keep watch
on all men's doing where it touches you,
their speech, and most of all, their discontents.
Your presence frightens any common man   690
from saying things you would not care to hear.
But in dark corners I have heard them say

how the whole town is grieving for this girl,
unjustly doomed, if ever woman was,
to die in shame for glorious action done.
She would not leave her fallen, slaughtered brother
there, as he lay, unburied, for the birds
and hungry dogs to make an end of him.
Isn't her real desert a golden prize?
This is the undercover speech in town.   700
Father, your welfare is my greatest good.
What loveliness in life for any child
outweighs a father's fortune and good fame?
And so a father feels his children's faring.
Then, do not have one mind, and one alone
that only your opinion can be right.
Whoever thinks that he alone is wise,
his eloquence, his mind, above the rest,
come the unfolding, shows his emptiness.
A man, though wise, should never be ashamed   710
of learning more, and must unbend his mind.
Have you not seen the trees beside the torrent,
the ones that bend them saving every leaf,
while the resistant perish root and branch?
And so the ship that will not slacken sail,
the sheet drawn tight, unyielding, overturns.
She ends the voyage with her keel on top.
No, yield your wrath, allow a change of stand.
Young as I am, if I may give advice,
I'd say it would be best if men were born   720
perfect in wisdom, but that failing this
(which often fails) it can be no dishonor
to learn from others when they speak good sense.

Chorus
Lord, if your son has spoken to the point
you should take his lesson. He should do the same.
Both sides have spoken well.

Creon
At my age I'm to school my mind by his?
This boy instructor is my master, then?

Haemon
I urge no wrong. I'm young, but you should watch
my actions, not my years, to judge of me.

Creon
A loyal action, to respect disorder? 730

Haemon
I wouldn't urge respect for wickedness.

Creon
You don't think she is sick with that disease?

Haemon
Your fellow-citizens maintain she's not.

Creon
Is the town to tell me how I ought to rule?

Haemon
Now there you speak just like a boy yourself.

Creon
Am I to rule by other mind than mine?

Haemon
No city is property of a single man.

Creon
But custom gives possession to the ruler.

Haemon
You'd rule a desert beautifully alone.

Creon (to the Chorus)
It seems he's firmly on the woman's side. 740

Haemon
If you're a woman. It is you I care for.

Creon
Wicked, to try conclusions with your father.

Haemon
When you conclude unjustly, so I must.

Creon
Am I unjust, when I respect my office?

Haemon
You tread down the gods' due. Respect is gone.

Creon
Your mind is poisoned. Weaker than a woman!

Haemon
At least you'll never see me yield to shame.

Creon
Your whole long argument is but for her.

Haemon
And you, and me, and for the gods below.

Creon
You shall not marry her while she's alive.   750

Haemon
Then she shall die. Her death will bring another.

Creon
Your boldness has made progress. Threats, indeed!

Haemon
No threat, to speak against your empty plan.

Creon
Past due, sharp lessons for your empty brain.

Haemon
If you weren't father, I should call you mad.

Creon
Don't flatter me with "father," you woman's slave.

Haemon
You wish to speak but never wish to hear.

Creon
You think so? By Olympus, you shall not
revile me with these tauntings and go free.
Bring out the hateful creature; she shall die
full in his sight, close at her bridegroom's side.   760

Haemon
Not at my side her death, and you will not
ever lay eyes upon my face again.
Find other friends to rave with after this.

(Haemon leaves, by one of the side entrances.)

Chorus
Lord, he has gone with all the speed of rage.
When such a man is grieved his mind is hard.

Creon
Oh, let him go, plan superhuman action.
In any case the girls shall not escape.

Chorus
You plan for both the punishment of death?   770

Creon
Not her who did not do it. You are right.

Chorus
And what death have you chosen for the other?

Creon
To take her where the foot of man comes not.
There shall I hide her in a hollowed cave
living, and leave her just so much to eat
as clears the city from the guilt of death.
There, if she prays to Death, the only god
of her respect, she may manage not to die.
Or she may learn at last and even then
how much too much her labor for the dead.   780

(Creon returns to the palace.)

Chorus
Love unconquered in fight, love who falls on our
    havings.
You rest in the bloom of a girl's unwithered face.
You cross the sea, you are known in the wildest lairs.
Not the immortal gods can fly,
nor men of a day. Who has you within him is mad.   790

You twist the minds of the just. Wrong they pursue
    and are ruined.
You made this quarrel of kindred before us now.
Desire looks clear from the eyes of a lovely bride:
power as strong as the founded world.
For there is the goddess at play with whom no man
    can fight.   800

(Antigone is brought from the palace under guard.)

Now I am carried beyond all bounds.
My tears will not be checked.
I see Antigone depart
to the chamber where all men sleep.

Antigone
Men of my fathers' land, you see me go
my last journey. My last sight of the sun,

then never again. Death who brings all to sleep   810
takes me alive to the shore
of the river underground.
Not for me was the marriage-hymn, nor will anyone
    start the song
at a wedding of mine. Acheron is my mate.

Chorus
    With praise as your portion you go
    in fame to the vault of the dead.
    Untouched by wasting disease,
    not paying the price of the sword,   820
    of your own motion you go.
    Alone among mortals will you descend
    in life to the house of Death.

Antigone
Pitiful was the death that stranger died,
our queen once, Tantalus' daughter. The rock
it covered her over, like stubborn ivy it grew.
Still, as she wastes, the rain
and snow companion her.
Pouring down from her mourning eyes comes the
    water that soaks the stone.   830
My own putting to sleep a god has planned like hers.

Chorus
    God's child and god she was.
    We are born to death.
    Yet even in death you will have your fame,
    to have gone like a god to your fate,
    in living and dying alike.

Antigone
Laughter against me now. In the name of our fathers'
    gods,
could you not wait till I went? Must affront be thrown
    in my face?   840
O city of wealthy men.
I call upon Dirce's spring,

I call upon Thebe's grove in the armored plain,
to be my witnesses, how with no friend's mourning,
by what decree I go to the fresh-made prison-tomb.
Alive to the place of corpses, an alien still,   850
never at home with the living nor with the dead.

Chorus

You went to the furthest verge
of daring, but there you found
the high foundation of justice, and fell.
Perhaps you are paying your father's pain.

Antigone

You speak of my darkest thought, my pitiful father's
    fame,
spread through all the world, and the doom that
    haunts our house,   860
the royal house of Thebes.
My mother's marriage-bed.
Destruction where she lay with her husband-son,
my father. These are my parents and I their child.
I go to stay with them. My curse is to die unwed.
My brother, you found your fate when you found
    your bride,   870
found it for me as well. Dead, you destroy my life.

Chorus

You showed respect for the dead.
So we for you: but power
is not to be thwarted so.
Your self-sufficiency has brought you down.

Antigone

Unwept, no wedding-song, unfriended, now I go
the road laid down for me.
No longer shall I see this holy light of the sun.   880
No friend to bewail my fate.

                    (*Creon enters from the palace.*)

Creon

When people sing the dirge for their own deaths
ahead of time, nothing will break them off
if they can hope that this will buy delay.
Take her away at once, and open up
the tomb I spoke of. Leave her there alone.
There let her choose: death, or a buried life.
No stain of guilt upon us in this case,
but she is exiled from our life on earth.   890

Antigone

O tomb, O marriage-chamber, hollowed out
house that will watch forever, where I go.
To my own people, who are mostly there;
Persephone has taken them to her.
Last of them all, ill-fated past the rest,
shall I descend, before my course is run.
Still when I get there I may hope to find
I come as a dear friend to my dear father,
to you, my mother, and my brother too.
All three of you have known my hand in death.   900
I washed your bodies, dressed them for the grave,
poured out the last libation at the tomb.
Last, Polyneices knows the price I pay
for doing final service to his corpse.
And yet the wise will know my choice was right.
Had I had children or their father dead,
I'd let them moulder. I should not have chosen
in such a case to cross the state's decree.
What is the law that lies behind these words?
One husband gone, I might have found another,
or a child from a new man in first child's place.   910
but with my parents hid away in death,
no brother, ever, could spring up for me.
Such was the law by which I honored you.
But Creon thought the doing was a crime,
a dreadful daring, brother of my heart.
So now he takes and leads me out by force.
No marriage-bed, no marriage-song for me,

and since no wedding, so no child to rear.
I go, without a friend, struck down by fate,
live to the hollow chambers of the dead.   920
What divine justice have I disobeyed?
Why, in my misery, look to the gods for help?
Can I call any of them my ally?
I stand convicted of impiety,
the evidence my pious duty done.
Should the gods think that this is righteousness,
in suffering I'll see my error clear.
But if it is the others who are wrong
I wish them no greater punishment than mine.

Chorus
    The same tempest of mind
    as ever, controls the girl.   930

Creon
    Therefore her guards shall regret
    the slowness with which they move.

Antigone
    That word comes close to death.

Creon
    You are perfectly right in that.

Antigone
    O town of my fathers in Thebe's land,
    O gods of our house.
    I am led away at last.
    Look, leaders of Thebes,   940
    I am last of your royal line.
    Look what I suffer, at whose command,
    because I respected the right.

    (Antigone is led away. The slow procession should
        begin during the preceding passage.)

Chorus
Danaë suffered too.
She went from the light to the brass-built room,
chamber and tomb together. Like you, poor child,
she was of great descent, and more, she held and kept
the seed of the golden rain which was Zeus.   950
Fate has terrible power.
You cannot escape it by wealth or war.
No fort will keep it out, no ships outrun it.

Remember the angry king,
son of Dryas, who raged at the god and paid,
pent in a rock-walled prison. His bursting wrath
slowly went down. As the terror of madness went,
he learned of his frenzied attack on the god.   960
Fool, he had tried to stop
the dancing women possessed of god,
the fire of Dionysus, the songs and flutes.

Where the dark rocks divide
sea from sea in Thrace
is Salmydessus whose savage god   970
beheld the terrible blinding wounds
dealt to Phineus' sons by their father's wife.
Dark the eyes that looked to avenge their mother.
Sharp with her shuttle she struck, and blooded her
    hands.

Wasting they wept their fate,
settled when they were born   980
to Cleopatra, unhappy queen.
She was a princess too, of an ancient house,
reared in the cave of the wild north wind, her father.
Half a goddess but, child, she suffered like you.

        (*Enter, from the side Teiresias, the blind prophet,
                        led by a boy attendant.*)

Teiresias
Elders of Thebes, we two have come one road,

two of us looking through one pair of eyes.
This is the way of walking for the blind. 990

Creon
Teiresias, what news has brought you here?

Teiresias
I'll tell you. You in turn must trust the prophet.

Creon
I've always been attentive to your counsel.

Teiresias
And therefore you have steered this city straight.

Creon
So I can say how helpful you have been.

Teiresias
But now you are balanced on a razor's edge.

Creon
What is it? How I shudder at your words!

Teiresias
You'll know, when you hear the signs that I have
    marked.
I sat where every bird of heaven comes 1000
in my old place of augury, and heard
bird-cries I'd never known. They screeched about
goaded by madness, inarticulate.
I marked that they were tearing one another
with claws of murder. I could hear the wing-beats.
I was afraid, so straight away I tried
burnt sacrifice upon the flaming altar.
No fire caught my offerings. Slimy ooze
dripped on the ashes, smoked and sputtered there.
Gall burst its bladder, vanished into vapor; 1010
the fat dripped from the bones and would not burn.

These are the omens of the rites that failed,
as my boy here has told me. He's my guide
as I am guide to others.
Why has this sickness struck against the state?
Through your decision.
All of the altars of the town are choked
with leavings of the dogs and birds; their feast
was on that fated, fallen Polyneices.
So the gods will have no offering from us,
not prayer, nor flame of sacrifice. The birds   1020
will not cry out a sound I can distinguish,
gorged with the greasy blood of that dead man.
Think of these things, my son. All men may err
but error once committed, he's no fool
nor yet unfortunate, who gives up his stiffness
and cures the trouble he has fallen in.
Stubbornness and stupidity are twins.
Yield to the dead. Why goad him where he lies?
What use to kill the dead a second time?   1030
I speak for your own good. And I am right.
Learning from a wise counsellor is not pain
if what he speaks are profitable words.

Creon

Old man, you all, like bowmen at a mark,
have bent your bows at me. I've had my share
of seers. I've been an item in your accounts.
Make profit, trade in Lydian silver-gold,
pure gold of India; that's your chief desire.
But you will never cover up that corpse.
Not if the very eagles tear their food   1040
from him, and leave it at the throne of Zeus.
I wouldn't give him up for burial
in fear of that pollution. For I know
no mortal being can pollute the gods.
O old Teiresias, human beings fall:
tho clever ones the furthest, when they plead
a shameful case so well in hope of profit.

Teiresias
Alas!
What man can tell me, has he thought at all . . .

Creon
What hackneyed saw is coming from your lips?

Teiresias
How better than all wealth is sound good counsel.   1050

Creon
And so is folly worse than anything.

Teiresias
And you're infected with that same disease.

Creon
I'm reluctant to be uncivil to a seer . . .

Teiresias
You're that already. You have said I lie.

Creon
Well, the whole crew of seers are money-mad.

Teiresias
And the whole tribe of tyrants grab at gain.

Creon
Do you realize you are talking to a king?

Teiresias
I know. Who helped you save this town you hold?

Creon
You're a wise seer, but you love wickedness.

Teiresias
You'll bring me to speak the unspeakable, very soon.   1060

Creon
Well, speak it out. But do not speak for profit.

Teiresias
No, there's no profit in my words for you.

Creon
You'd better realise that you can't deliver
my mind, if you should sell it, to the buyer.

Teiresias
Know well, the sun will not have rolled its course
many more days, before you come to give
corpse for these corpses, child of your own loins.
For you've confused the upper and lower worlds.
You sent a life to settle in a tomb;
you keep up here that which belongs below   1070
the corpse unburied, robbed of its release.
Not you, nor any god that rules on high
can claim him now.
You rob the nether gods of what is theirs.
So the pursuing horrors lie in wait
to track you down. The Furies sent by Hades
and by all gods will even you with your victims.
Now say that I am bribed! At no far time
shall men and women wail within your house.
And all the cities that you fought in war   1080
whose sons had burial from wild beasts, or dogs,
or birds that brought the stench of your great wrong
back to each hearth, they move against you now.
A bowman, as you said, I send my shafts,
now you have moved me, straight. You'll feel the
   wound.
Boy, take me home now. Let him spend his rage
on younger men, and learn to calm his tongue,
and keep a better mind than now he does.   1090

                                          (*Exit.*)

Chorus

Lord, he has gone. Terrible prophecies!
And since the time when I first grew gray hair
his sayings to the city have been true.

Creon

I also know this. And my mind is torn.
To yield is dreadful. But to stand against him.
Dreadful to strike my spirit to destruction.

Chorus

Now you must come to counsel, and take advice.

Creon

What must I do? Speak, and I shall obey.

Chorus

Go free the maiden from that rocky house.   1100
Bury the dead who lies in readiness.

Creon

This is your counsel? You would have me yield?

Chorus

Quick as you can. The gods move very fast
when they bring ruin on misguided men.

Creon

How hard, abandonment of my desire.
But I can fight necessity no more.

Chorus

Do it yourself. Leave it to no one else.

Creon

I'll go at once. Come, followers, to your work.
You that are here round up the other fellows.
Take axes with you, hurry to that place
that overlooks us.   1110

Now my decision has been overturned
shall I, who bound her, set her free myself.
I've come to fear it's best to hold the laws
of old tradition to the end of life.

(*Exit.*)

Chorus
God of the many names, Semele's golden child,
child of Olympian thunder, Italy's lord.
Lord of Eleusis, where all men come   1120
to mother Demeter's plain.
Bacchus, who dwell in Thebes,
by Ismenus' running water,
where wild Bacchic women are at home,
on the soil of the dragon seed.

Seen in the glaring flame, high on the double mount,
with the nymphs of Parnassus at play on the hill,
seen by Kastalia's flowing stream.   1130
You come from the ivied heights,
from green Euboea's shore.
In immortal words we cry
your name, lord, who watch the ways,
the many ways of Thebes.

This is your city, honored beyond the rest,
the town of your mother's miracle-death.
Now, as we wrestle our grim disease,   1140
come with healing step from Parnassus' slope
or over the moaning sea.

Leader in dance of the fire-pulsing stars,
overseer of the voices of night,
child of Zeus, be manifest,
with due companionship of Maenad maids   1150
whose cry is but your name.

(*Enter one of those who left with Creon,
as messenger.*)

Messenger
Neighbors of Cadmus, and Amphion's house,
there is no kind of state in human life
which I now dare to envy or to blame.
Luck sets it straight, and luck she overturns
the happy or unhappy day by day
No prophecy can deal with men's affairs.   1160
Creon was envied once, as I believe,
for having saved this city from its foes
and having got full power in this land.
He steered it well. And he had noble sons.
Now everything is gone.
Yes, when a man has lost all happiness,
he's not alive. Call him a breathing corpse.
Be very rich at home. Live as a king.
But once your joy has gone, though these are left
they are smoke's shadow to lost happiness.   1170

Chorus
What is the grief of princes that you bring?

Messenger
They're dead. The living are responsible.

Chorus
Who died? Who did the murder? Tell us now.

Messenger
Haemon is gone. One of his kin drew blood.

Chorus
But whose arm struck? His father's or his own?

Messenger
He killed himself. His blood is on his father.

Chorus
Seer, all too true the prophecy you told!

Messenger
This is the state of things. Now make your plans.

(Enter, from the palace, Eurydice.)

Chorus
Eurydice is with us now, I see.   1180
Creon's poor wife. She may have come by chance.
She may have heard something about her son.

Eurydice
I heard your talk as I was coming out
to greet the goddess Pallas with my prayer.
And as I moved the bolts that held the door
I heard of my own sorrow.
I fell back fainting in my women's arms.
But say again just what the news you bring.   1190
I, whom you speak to, have known grief before.

Messenger
Dear lady, I was there, and I shall tell,
leaving out nothing of the true account.
Why should I make it soft for you with tales
to prove myself a liar? Truth is right.
I followed your husband to the plain's far edge,
where Polyneices' corpse was lying still
unpitied. The dogs had torn him all apart.   1200
We prayed the goddess of all journeyings,
and Pluto, that they turn their wrath to kindness,
we gave the final purifying bath,
then burned the poor remains on new-cut boughs,
and heaped a high mound of his native earth.
Then turned we to the maiden's rocky bed,
death's hollow marriage-chamber.
But, still far off, one of us heard a voice
in keen lament by that unblest abode.
He ran and told the master. As Creon came
he heard confusion crying. He groaned and spoke: 1210
"Am I a prophet now, and do I tread
the saddest of all roads I ever trod?

My son's voice crying! Servants, run up close,
stand by the tomb and look, push through the crevice
where we built the pile of rock, right to the entry.
Find out if that is Haemon's voice I hear
or if the gods are tricking me indeed."
We obeyed the order of our mournful master.
In the far corner of the tomb we saw   1220
her, hanging by the neck, caught in a noose
of her own linen veiling.
Haemon embraced her as she hung, and mourned
his bride's destruction, dead and gone below,
his father's actions, the unfated marriage.
When Creon saw him, he groaned terribly,
and went toward him, and called him with lament:
"What have you done, what plan have you caught up,
what sort of suffering is killing you?
Come out, my child, I do beseech you, come!"   1230
The boy looked at him with his angry eyes,
spat in his face and spoke no further word.
He drew his sword, but as his father ran,
he missed his aim. Then the unhappy boy,
in anger at himself, leant on the blade.
It entered, half its length, into his side.
While he was conscious he embraced the maiden,
holding her gently. Last, he gasped out blood,
red blood on her white cheek.
Corpse on a corpse he lies. He found his marriage.   1240
Its celebration in the halls of Hades.
So he has made it very clear to men
that to reject good counsel is a crime.

              (*Eurydice returns to the house.*)

Chorus
What do you make of this? The queen has gone
in silence. We know nothing of her mind.

Messenger
I wonder at her, too. But we can hope
that she has gone to mourn her son within

with her own women, not before the town.
She knows discretion. She will do no wrong.   1250

Chorus
I am not sure. This muteness may portend
as great disaster as a loud lament.

Messenger
I will go in and see if some deep plan
hides in her heart's wild pain. You may be right.
There can be heavy danger in mute grief.

(*The messenger goes into the house. Creon enters
with his followers. They are carrying
Haemon's body on a bier.*)

Chorus
But look, the king draws near.
His own hand brings
the witness of his crime,
the doom he brought on himself.   1260

Creon
O crimes of my wicked heart,
harshness bringing death.
You see the killer, you see the kin he killed.
My planning was all unblest.
Son, you have died too soon.
Oh, you have gone away
through my fault, not your own.

Chorus
You have learned justice, though it comes too late.   1270

Creon
Yes, I have learned in sorrow. It was a god who
   struck,
who has weighted my head with disaster; he drove
   me to wild strange ways,

his heavy heel on my joy.
Oh sorrows, sorrows of men.

*(Re-enter the messenger, from a side door
of the palace.)*

Messenger
Master, you hold one sorrow in your hands
but you have more, stored up inside the house.   1280

Creon
What further suffering can come on me?

Messenger
Your wife has died. The dead man's mother in deed,
poor soul, her wounds are fresh.

Creon
Hades, harbor of all,
you have destroyed me now.
Terrible news to hear, horror the tale you tell.   1290
I was dead, and you kill me again.
Boy, did I hear you right?
Did you say the queen was dead,
slaughter on slaughter heaped?

(The central doors of the palace begin to open.)

Chorus
Now you can see. Concealment is all over.

*(The doors are open, and the corpse of Eurydice
is revealed.)*

Creon
My second sorrow is here. Surely no fate remains
which can strike me again. Just now, I held my son
  in my arms.
And now I see her dead.
Woe for the mother and son.   1300

Messenger
There, by the altar, dying on the sword,
her eyes fell shut. She wept her older son
who died before, and this one. Last of all
she cursed you as the killer of her children.

Creon
I am mad with fear. Will no one strike
and kill me with cutting sword?
Sorrowful, soaked in sorrow to the bone!   1310

Messenger
Yes, for she held you guilty in the death
of him before you, and the elder dead.

Creon
How did she die?

Messenger
                         Struck home at her own heart
when she had heard of Haemon's suffering.

Creon
This is my guilt, all mine. I killed you, I say it clear.
Servants, take me away, out of the sight of men.   1320
I who am nothing more than nothing now.

Chorus
Your plan is good—if any good is left.
Best to cut short our sorrow.

Creon
Let me go, let me go. May death come quick,
bringing my final day.   1330
O let me never see tomorrow's dawn.

Chorus
That is the future's. We must look to now.
What will be is in other hands than ours.

Creon
All my desire was in that prayer of mine.

Chorus
Pray not again. No mortal can escape
the doom prepared for him.

Creon
Take me away at once, the frantic man who killed   1340
my son, against my meaning. I cannot rest.
My life is warped past curse. My fate has struck me
    down.

(Creon and his attendants enter the house.)

Chorus
What will be is in other hands than ours.
    Our happiness depends
    on wisdom all the way.
    The gods must have their due.
    Great words by men of pride   1350
    bring greater blows upon them.
    So wisdom comes to the old.

A NOTE ON THE TEXT

The foregoing is a translation of the text of Jebb's third edition (Cambridge, 1900). In the dialogue, I have tried to bring into English almost all that I thought I saw in the Greek, even though this was to run the risk of a clumsy literalism. In the choruses, I have taken more freedom.

The following are the places where my rendering is of another text than Jebb's.

486. ὁμαιμονεστέρας A, other MSS, and the scholiast in L. ὁμαιμονεστέρα L, as corrected from -αις, Jebb.

The extravagance of imagining the impossible possibility of closer blood kin than a sister seems to me in character for Creon at this point. (For a similar use of language, cf. Aeschylus *Septem* 197.)

519. τούτους MSS and Jebb. ἴσους is recorded by L's scholiast and read by Pearson. Line 520 seems even more pointed if Creon is picking up Antigone's own term to throw at her.

572. This line is Ismene's in all the manuscripts. The only traditional evidence for giving it to Antigone is that the Aldine edition (1502) and Turnebus (1553) gave it to her. These editors may have had manuscript evidence lost to us. But they may also, like most modern editors, including Jebb, have been exercising their own sense of fitness. It is touching to have an Antigone stung from her silence to defend her lover. Further, if the line is not hers, we are faced with

an Antigone who never mentions him; and much has been built on this.

The best argument for giving her the line is Creon's reply to it (573). If Ismene has 572 "your marriage" must mean "the marriage you talk of," or words to that effect. This is possible, but the phrase would certainly come out more naturally to Antigone.

Confusions of speakers in stichomythia are many, and I see no possibility of certainty here. It is our misfortune that the line in question is an important one. I have stayed with the manuscripts, which seems to me all one can do.

574. This is Ismene's line in all MSS. Boeckh, followed by Jebb, gave it to the chorus. I have followed my own precedent in 572, and stayed with the MSS. The question might come, as Jebb argues, more reasonably from the chorus than from Ismene, who has had her answer already. But she is not too logical to ask the same appalling question twice.

600. κόνις MSS, Jebb. κοπίς Reiske and others, Jebb in earlier editions, Pearson. See Jebb's note and appendix. He was of two minds here. My own final feeling is that for dust to be doing the reaping is too much, even for a tragic chorus.

609. παντογήρως L, the MSS generally, L's scholiast. παντ' ἀγρεύων, Jebb. This image was too strained for Jebb (and many others), as the dust in 600 was for me. De gustibus. . . .

904–20. Jebb (following and followed by many) brackets these lines, which are in all the MSS, and were known to Aristotle as Antigone's. I think he is wrong, but he should not be pilloried as a prudish Victorian for this. The positions of his note and appendix are well taken and held. Some sensible contemporaries (e.g., Fitts and Fitzgerald) are with him still. For those, like myself, who are sure the lines are Antigone's, there is drama in her abandoning her moralities and clinging to her irrational profundity of feeling for her lost and irreplaceable brother, devising legalistic arguments

for her intellectual justification. Jebb finds the syntax of
909–12 strained past all bearing, but I believe Antigone's
obscurity here a touch of realism parallel to the confused
and contradictory negatives of her opening lines, which
Jebb allows her.